# CHAKRA AND CRYSTALS FOR BEGINNERS

*A COMPLETE GUIDE TO CRYSTALS AND HEALING STONES. DISCOVER HOW TO HEAL YOUR BODY AND BALANCE YOUR CHAKRAS, INCLUDING SECRET TIPS TO THE THIRD EYE AWAKENING.*

# Table of Contents

# Introduction

Humankind has always been on an unending quest for energy. We are an energy-hungry species. We have always tried to harness and exploit energy in every form possible. The biggest wars fought on this planet have been energy wars are they are still going on in latent forms. However, while we looked for energy and power all around us, most of us never bothered to look inwards.

Our body is a big pool of energy that can help us in achieving unimaginable feats. Although we have been busy looking for the answers for most of our mental, emotional, and physical problems outside, they can easily be resolved with the help of these energies.

Chakras are the reservoirs of energy in our body. If the chakras in our body are balanced and functioning, we can run up to our full potential and even do things that might look impossible at the moment. However, if these energy centers are blocked or unbalanced, they will only cause damage and stop our progress.

The modern way of living has become such that imbalance in chakras is common. Increase strife among individuals, psychological issues, emotional turbulence, and the chaos in relationships is a result of such imbalances. If you can devote some time to understand the importance of chakras and their imbalance in the body, you will be able to overcome most of such problems in life very easily. What might look totally unconnected is sometimes very intricately intertwined.

This book will help you in understanding the concept of the Chakra System and how it affects your life.

This book will prove to be a comprehensive guide for the main 7 chakras in your body and explain the ways in which they affect your life. You will get to know in detail their functions and the problems that can arise due to an imbalance in any particular chakra.

It will give you an in-depth knowledge of the ways in which the chakras work. You will also get to know their effect on your mental, physical, emotional, as well as spiritual well being.

This book will explain the various states of chakras in your body. It will show you the benefits of open chakras that allow a smooth flow of energy. It will also explain the impact of closed, blocked, and overactive chakras on your body. You will get to know the symptoms and ailments that can be caused due to chakra imbalance.

This book will provide you in-depth knowledge about chakra healing and the impact it will have on you. You will get to know various ways to do chakra healing so that you can find the best fit for you. It isn't something in which one solution fits all. That's why this book brings to you various effective ways that can be used for chakra healing so that you can choose the medium that suits you the most.

The concept of chakras may look ancient and unscientific but it is a wisdom that is precious. This eastern practice of chakra healing can help you in finding your lost balance that may be troubling you in your daily life. It will help you in finding your peace. You will feel more grounded in reality. Pursuing your dreams would become easier as your energies would be helping you.

All this can be achieved with the help of some simple practices. This book doesn't bring to you complex practices or methods but would help you in doing all this with some simple techniques.

# Chapter 1 Introducing chakra

In order to understand how to awaken your chakras, you must first understand what and how important they are. Chakras, or cakra as they are known in some countries, are energy centers within your body. The concept of chakras goes back hundreds of years; the very first discussion about Chakras originated in India between 1500 B.C and 500 B.C in a text called Vedas. But it was also mentioned in countless other texts, such as the Yoga-Shikka Upanishad, the Shri Jabala Darshana Upanishad, and the Shandilya Upanishad. It wasn't until a scholar Anodea Judith wrote a book titled 'Wheels of Life' in 1987 that the concept of chakras was brought to Europe. Since then, more New Age authors have written books about chakras to the point that the idea of energy centers is universally understood.

You now know where the idea of chakras originated, but what are they really? Chakras are specific energies within your body, and they each have their own functions, color, and vibrational frequency that can affect a person in different ways. Together they are the energetic blueprint for our bodies. Energy can't be destroyed or created, as Einstein said, but it is there, flowing inside our bodies and everywhere around us. We are all energies, and the chakra points are where most of our energy is centered, together they are able to keep us psychologically, physically, emotionally and spiritually balanced. However, most of the time that balance gets tipped, and people become either too engrossed in something or show no care in the world for it.

Each of the chakras applies its energy differently in our lives, but they are all emotionally related, which is why having the wrong mindset can cause illnesses and diseases within the body. The root chakra refers to your understanding of the words 'I exist,' meaning the ability to enjoy life and know what makes your time on earth special. The sacral chakra embodies 'I desire,' which means that it is not selfish to wish for something that you deeply want; in fact, you should have plenty desires as long as you make sure they are not negative. The solar plexus chakra refers to your destiny with the words 'I control,' in that only you can shape your own future and destiny; there is no book in the world that tells you how you should act or what you should do because that power belongs to you and only you. With the words 'I love' from the heart chakra, you are fully able to spread love to yourself and others. The throat chakra refers to the words 'I express,' meaning you have the ability to say whatever is on your mind. The third eye chakra, 'I am the witness,' gives you the power to warn yourself of things that happen in your life with the gift of intuition.

Throughout life, many of our chakra points become blocked or imbalanced and it is up to us to revitalize them once more. For example, if your heart chakra is blocked, it can strongly affect your relationships with people around you. You might experience trust issues, or be unable to let go of a past relationship. This is caused by dwelling on bad memories, overthinking, or traumas from past relationships. This blocked energy will make it difficult for you to make and build new relationships with people. If you want to be happy, you have to let your heart open to all the possibilities around you, to the new relationships that you will form, and to the old ones that you can mend. This will make you truly happy.

The process of awakening chakras can be difficult. When awakening a chakra, you may feel weak, stressed, nervous, and shaken up because the energy is flowing through you and releasing all the negative thoughts, habits and behavior. Its purpose is to heal your body and remove all the toxins in order to leave you feeling happy, loved, cared for, fearless, calm, and lively. It can even increase the healing process of your physical, emotional, mental and spiritual states.

There are many benefits from awakening our chakras. By now you know that a blocked chakra can create disease or illness in the body, but a healthy chakra also has the power to heal the body. The effects are not only physical but can be in the mental realm, as opening a chakra can help you form healthy habits and behaviors. Many people may experience an increase in strength in their physical bodies, such as finding they are able to run for longer distances when exercising. But there are some people who experience a knowledge awakening, perhaps feeling they suddenly have answers to things they don't recall reading or learning about. The energies of the universe are truly a mysterious power!

We can manipulate this power to our advantage using our chakras. One way of doing this is by mastering the healing energy of Reiki, and another is by awakening the kundalini power in your root chakra.

The practice of Reiki is a healing form of energy that originated in Japan, discovered by a Buddhist monk by the name of Mikao Usui who was able to understand the energy that flows through every living being and how to channel such a force. It is known to reduce stress and anxiety as well as promote healing of all kinds, mind, body, spirit, and emotions. 'Rei' means god's wisdom and the higher power, while 'Ki' means life force energy. Together it is the spiritually-guided life force energy. Reiki can help you clear your energy and awaken your chakras, because it clears any blocks and helps turn the negative energy-form diseases into positive and pure energy. There are five Reiki principles or guides on how to live your life to the fullest with happiness, health, and love. They are:

"Just for today, I will not worry."

"Just for today, I will not be angry."

"Just for today, I will be grateful."

"Just for today, I will do my work honestly."

"Just for today, I will be kind to every living thing."

You repeat to yourself these five principles every morning, or you can say them after you've completed your daily meditation. There are many teachers and practitioners of Reiki, and you can even find a local teacher who can help you learn how to harness the Reiki healing energy. If you happen to not have any Reiki practitioners nearby, there are many teachers online who can help you channel the energies. You might be wondering, how could it work if the healer is nowhere near me? And the answer to that is that Reiki energy has no boundaries when it comes to time and space; it is all about your intentions through the long-distance sessions.

Reiki is a pure form of healing that does not require talent or years of practice. When performing a Reiki healing, you are opening up your crown, heart, and palm chakras to heal yourself and others around you.

There are three main levels of Reiki healing. We begin with Reiki I, who are just beginners and practitioners who are practicing on themselves. Reiki II can use the first three Reiki symbols (sacred shapes imbued with meaning) and can perform over long distances, while Reiki III which is the master who is able to heal those through distance, to use all the Reiki symbols, and is able to help others open their Reiki. You can learn to heal yourself and others around you whether it is through distance or face-to-face with the power of Reiki healing. It is a safe and gentle practice, so you have nothing to worry about. You can get a master or teacher of Reiki to help you open your energy or you can do it at home by following the steps below.

First, you start by connecting with the Reiki energy with the power of invocations by calling out to the universe. You are reaching out to the universal energy and asking for the power of healing. Take a few minutes to meditate, relaxing your body and mind before you proceed. You can make up your own invocation, which will have more effect because it will come from your heart and own beliefs. Below is a brief example.

Form your hands into a mudra (position of palms touching in front of you), close your eyes, and visualize the energy of the universe flowing into your hands with a bluish-white light as it surrounds you. Feel the energy spreading through your body. Details of the Universal light are not important, since there are practitioners of Reiki who cannot see the light while others can.

The next step is to set your healing intentions through a message to the body of what you want to heal. You are just making a note inside your head that you want to heal something and then visualizing how you would feel if it was truly healed. For example, if you have an injured arm, don't focus a lot of attention on how you would feel if it was healed but more of how happy you would be being able to do the things you require of that hand.

Imagine that you have placed your intentions into your hands. Focus on bringing the healing energy to your hands, feeling the warmth or tingling sensations before placing them on yourself.

If it's a knee pain you wish to go away then place both hands, on top of each other, on your knee. Focus on transmitting that energy to your knee, visualize it healing your knee and repeating an intention for it to be healed. Feel the warmth of your skin and imagine healing it. You can also use Reiki symbols, but focusing energy through symbols is a bit more challenging and is only used by practitioners who are on level two and above. There are also many free sessions online and on YouTube that you can follow, which prove to be very helpful and beneficial.

After performing a Reiki healing, you might start to feel tingling or warm sensations throughout your body, signaling that the energy is flowing through you. Since Reiki has the ability to heal, you will feel energy concentrated in different points of your chakras. Emotionally, you might find yourself wanting to cry or laugh, letting go of past feelings that you kept bubbling up inside of you without your awareness signifies the healing approach of Reiki. You can even see visions or messages pop into your head, warnings or advice that is meant to help you throughout your journey. This can help you clear any karma that you might be receiving in your life!

The kundalini awakening concerns a form of energy that is located at the base of the spine. To understand what that is, you must first understand that your soul has chosen your body and come down to earth for a reason and if you are not fulfilling that purpose, the kundalini power can turn into a disruptive energy in order to urge you to change your course. It acts as a reminder that you should be doing something different, something better. The kundalini is the energy of our awareness or attention, it manifests with the consciousness when it becomes free from your thoughts, which is why meditation can awaken the kundalini. When awakened, this energy flows freely through the seven chakras, opening all the seven chakras at the same time which expands the consciousness further. For people who experience the awakening, their whole ground and reality shifts, they begin to feel different and their perception of the world around them changes. It can be a terrifying experience for some because it is a powerful force of nature that is completely different from ordinary life, and the body, mind, and spirit are not used to being exposed to such high energy and power.

For many people, the kundalini awakening can be rather beautiful, filled with feelings of love, and happiness. If done incorrectly, others may have feelings of depression, anxiety or discomfort. It is important to maintain a positive attitude if you want to heal yourself psychologically and physically; otherwise, you might become exposed to the dangerous side of kundalini. It takes years to awaken the kundalini for many practitioners, but the process changes them into a better and healthier version of themselves. There are many benefits for awakening kundalini, including developing psychic abilities, healing your physical body, gaining higher energy levels, creativity, and deep knowing, and even possibly slowing down the aging process.

Awakening the kundalini or the chakras can help heal your body from any diseases. If you are planning on attempting to awaken the kundalini, first awaken a few of your chakras, because your body needs to become familiar with the energy and so you will know what to expect. That energy will become magnified, however, and that energy won't leave you, so you have to become committed to dealing with such powers. There are also plenty of ways to awaken the kundalini but you have to be mindful, you have to be aware of what you are doing because that energy can also turn against you.

There are certain things that must be done before attempting to awaken the kundalini. You have to cleanse your body from any toxins by drinking plenty of water and eating healthy foods. You have to keep your body healthy; this means avoiding caffeine, junk food, alcohol, and smoking. Practicing and building your body in preparation for awakening is very beneficial. Different types of yoga such as hatha yoga, jnana yoga, bhakta, and kundalini yoga are very helpful, so look into each of them and find whichever one suits you the best.

Prepare your mind for this spiritual awakening. You have to purify your mind in order to prepare for dealing with the temptations that will follow after the energy is awakened. To do that, you have to step away from negativity. Focus on the positive things in life; it is scientifically proven that one positive thought is hundreds of times more powerful than a negative one. Being more positive and spreading love will attract more good things into your life; the universe rewards those who do good. A good way of achieving a positive mindset is meditation, which is also the key for this spiritual transformation.

Many people have experienced kundalini without knowing of it or being aware that they had awakened it. This happens because kundalini power is linked with the spiritual exercises such as meditation and yoga, which are often used to awaken the chakras.

By choosing to use this book as a resource, you are showing signs of an emotional reckoning. You may find yourself looking back at past experiences that make you feel sad or longing for the old days. You might experience heightened emotions, feel sad for no reason, or extremely happy when something good happens. You are starting to spend a lot of time figuring out how you came to be the way that you are, you are looking back at the past thinking about what happened and what you wish went differently, which is your perfect opportunity to come to peace with the situation and release it.

Your emotions change as your heart opens to more love and compassion. You begin to feel others' emotions and exactly what they are experiencing. This might become overwhelming at first because your emotions are tangling with those of others, but it is a positive sign that your third eye is being opened and that you are becoming more acquainted with your true nature. This happens because you are dealing with emotions that you have suppressed and bottled up, and now they are finally catching up with you. Nature will feel more welcoming, and you may have a strong urge to be outside as much as possible.

You will start waking up at random hours during the night, crying, sweating, or with intense energy rushing up and down your spine. Many people leave their jobs, relationships, or hometowns during their awakening because of the sudden need to change their life. You start to realize what isn't working in your life and what needs to go. You will notice that you are becoming more distant with some people, and close with others because of your strong sense that toxic relationships are holding you back from accomplishing your dreams. Your energy opens your eyes to the things that should be making you feel happy and not sad. Your mindset also starts to change because of the life energy force that has been awakened. You begin to understand things that you hadn't before, and living will start to make sense the further you go along your spiritual path. When you have awakened the power of your chakras, the universe will attract the solutions to your problems, and you will find yourself realizing that all your problems are 'magically' working themselves out, making you think that the world is in your favor.

You may start to question life, religion, and politics. Your viewpoints change and become more open; you will find yourself looking at things from a different perspective and learning things that never came to your mind before. A strong need to help others will guide you through the beginning of your days experiencing the kundalini, as you will feel compassion towards others and go out of your way to help the people around you.

Acceptance will soon replace the feelings of anger concerning how you lived before you experienced the kundalini, as all the pain that you suffered in life turns into acceptance that you have passed the hardest chapter of your life. Your thoughts turn into reality. What you were putting out into the world was what you were getting back but now you begin to feel a connection with life, yourself, and the divine. You recognize yourself as a piece of a god, as are the others around you. You have the power to change your life, and no one else has that divine power over you.

When you realize the urgency of finally living the life you've always dreamed about, you will start to put your power to the test and eliminate things that make you feel lesser. The kundalini is a beautiful awakening. It feels like this life you are living right now is just a dream, and when you experience the actual awakening, then you realize that you were just asleep all this time and that your life can begin now.

Just by wanting to read this book and learn more about awakening, you've already taken a big step in your spiritual path of acceptance of yourself and the world around you. You have the power and energy to heal yourself, and you can also ask the universe for guidance and those with the higher power to guide you. As soon as you make a connection with the universe, you will start to share that same power because together you are one. Don't be afraid of diving deeper into the inner wisdom to unlock the truth of your being here, and don't be afraid of the energy and the power that you can harness through awaking your chakra and kundalini. As long as you are able to keep a straight and positive mindset, the universe will look after you.

# Chapter 2 The 7 chakras and association

The word "chakra" frequently comes up when talking about self-healing. You may have heard someone talking about the 7 chakras, and how they can help your spiritual health and wellbeing. Oftentimes, however, people have different interpretations of what the 7 chakras mean and symbolize, which can be pretty confusing when attempting to learn about them. But what are the 7 chakras, and what does the word "chakra" mean anyway?

Before we start talking about chakras, we need to talk about energy. It's very easy to notice the energy, or life-force, that is ever-present in our world. For example, think about walking into a room and hearing a conversation between two people. You can probably pick up on the vibe in the room, whether it's tense or lighthearted. This is you sensing the energy in the room created by these two people. Alternately, think about how, after a conversation with some people, you feel drained, like they've sucked the life out of you. It could be that these people are stealing this energy from you.

Energy isn't just something that we people have. The universe is filled with it; plants, animals, and stones have energy as well. Everything contained within the universe is constantly exchanging and processing this energy, or life-force. It goes by a number of different names, including prana, chi, and ki.

There are three types of energetic fields that you have in and around your body. The first is your aura, an energy field surrounding you. The second is meridians, which are energy channels throughout your body. If you've ever done acupuncture, meridians are what acupuncturists use.

The third is what we'll be focusing on. These are chakras, or energy centers or portals in your body's energy field.

To start off our journey into the world of chakra healing, we must have an understanding of what chakras are. In this chapter, we'll provide an overview of each of the 7 chakras, learning about the location and attributes of each. But to begin with, we'll go over what a chakra actually is.

The word "chakra" is from the Sanskrit language, the ancient language of India, and is pronounced "chuhk-ruh." It means "wheel," which should give a hint as to what the 7 chakras are. Basically, you can visualize chakras as 7 centers of spiritual power and energy found in your body that are constantly spinning, like a wheel, driving life energy throughout your body. Each of the 7 chakras is located in a different place in your body, and drives a different part of your spiritual and physical experience.

You can think of it as a system for understanding the complex flows of life-force energy throughout your body. This system is based on thousands of years of observation and documentation.

It is the culmination of patterns we have noticed in ourselves since ancient times.

The chakras are located in a straight line, following your spine. This is because the chakras spin energy from Earth below to Heaven above. Starting from the bottom and the most material chakras, we move to the highest chakras, which are your connection to the divine.

Each of the 7 chakras is a step on the ladder between matter and consciousness, earth and heaven. Therefore, in learning about the chakras, we'll journey from energy related to material concerns, then to the more complex energies governing our interpersonal relationships, and finally to the more abstract concepts of the universal consciousness. When we understand the chakras and have balanced them all, we have crossed the bridge that connects Earth and Heaven, allowing ourselves to understand the all-encompassing nature of reality.

There are other chakras and chakra systems out there. However, it's common practice to begin with the 7-chakra system, as it is widely accepted as mapping the major chakras. Through modern physiology we can see that each of the 7 chakras is mapped onto one of the nerve ganglia, the nerve clusters that emanate from the spinal column. By mastering these chakra, which is difficult enough, you have the power to live a healthy and fulfilling life.

If you experience a perceived imbalance in your spiritual, emotional, or physical health, it could be because of a blocked or imbalanced chakra. This can result from a number of external or internal influences. Luckily, it is quite possible to unblock and balance your chakras through meditation and other methods.

Just because your chakras are clear and balanced doesn't mean that you won't experience stress and hardship in your life. It does, however, put you in the correct state of mind to handle situations as they arise.

When your energy is healthy, you too are healthy. When it's not, you can suffer from a range of ailments, both mental and physical.

The biggest thing to remember about your chakras is that you are in control! With practice, you'll be able to work with each of your chakras and skillfully bring each one to balance. Your intention in the most important thing. You have to truly will yourself to heal and be better in order for the healing process to take great effect.

The concept of chakras is a very old one, dating back thousands of years. They are first mentioned in a Hindu text, the "Yoga Kundalini Upanishad," dating back to 1400 B.C. Over time, our conception of chakras has evolved, until now we have arrived at the modern model of 7 chakras:

- Root Chakra, or "Muladhara"

- Sacral Chakra, or "Svadhisthana"

- Navel Chakra, or "Manipura"

- Heart Chakra, or "Anahata"

- Throat Chakra, or "Vishuddha"

- Third Eye Chakra, or "Ajna"

- Crown Chakra, or "Sahasrara"

These 7 chakras each align with a different point on the spinal cord, from the top of the head to the bottom of the spine. Each chakra has a symbol and a color of the rainbow associated with it, which is useful to know for reading chakra diagrams and for fully understanding each chakra. The lower five elements are also associated with the five classical elements: fire, earth, air, water, and aether, or space.

It is important to understand each of the symbols associated with each chakra, so pay attention! These symbols will continue to recur as the basis for a number of techniques for accessing, unblocking and balancing the chakras.

For a detailed breakdown of each of the 7 chakras, read on.

## Root Chakra

The Root Chakra, or "Muladhara," is found at the bottom of the spine. It is the first chakra in the list of seven, and the foundation of the chakra system.

It is often symbolized by a red lotus flower with four petals. As you'd imagine, its color is red. It has a connection with the element of earth; when you sit for meditation, this part of your body is touching the earth, which relates to the Root Chakra's role in grounding you.

The Root Chakra is the chakra that is houses the energy for security and stability in your life. It is also responsible for anchoring your energy in the earth and the material world. A foundation is a good way to think of the Root Chakra, because it anchors the higher chakras to the earth and the physical world. Balancing the Root Chakra is an important step for stabilizing the chakras above.

To that end, the Root Chakra is made up of what centers you in stability, or what are considered the four primal urges: food, self-preservation, sex, and sleep. When these urges are in balance in your life, this goes a long way toward balancing the Root Chakra as well. However, if you are experiencing pressure or stress in any of these areas, this may block or unbalance the Root Chakra.

The vital life force that is present in this chakra begins at conception, when the masculine and feminine energies of sperm and egg combine. It then continues with the life force energy dividing the cells during the process of Embryogenesis in the womb. The spinal column begins to develop from this point, after which organs develop.

When you balance this chakra, you feel secure, grounded, humble, stable, and energetic. You'll feel calm and secure about your place in the world, and will find it simpler for your inner self to connect to peace in every moment.

It's easy to tell a person who has a balanced root chakra. We usually describe this as having common sense. They use what they have to provide for their needs and are organized. They may decide to put their "root down" and choose one place to settle instead of living a vagabond lifestyle. They are close to their family and those who they love.

However, when this chakra is blocked, or restricting the energy flow throughout your body, you may be prone to feeling anxious and suspicious and withdrawing from others. It's also possible that you could have an overactive Root Chakra. In this case, you may be prone to hoarding, overworking, and greed, and anger. You may have problems accepting change and put too much value in material possessions.

Remember, in meditation and visualization, that this chakra spins downward, while chakras 2-6 spin in circles instead.

It is important to have a balanced Root Chakra to build that strong base on which a healthy and balanced system of chakras will be based.

## Sacral Chakra

The Sacral Chakra, or "Svadhisthana," is located at the pelvis, between your genitals and your navel. It is the second chakra in the list of seven.

This chakra is often represented by an orange lotus with six petals, and has a connection with the color orange. It is also associated with the element of water, which relates to the fluid, adaptable, and creative nature of this chakra.

Whereas the Root Chakra was focused on meeting your body's physical needs, the Sacral Chakra is much more tied into your body's emotional needs. This is where the energy is housed for satisfying your needs for human identity, emotion, and creativity. It helps you regulate your emotions and desires, instead of you being controlled by them.

This chakra provides you with something very vital; the force to enjoy life through the senses and your emotions. Whereas the Root Chakra was concerned with the physiological need for sex, this chakra supports you in the pursuit of sexual pleasure, as well as other pleasureable aspects of life, while maintaining a healthy balance. Opening the Sacral Chakra is also important for allowing you to feel the world around you to the fullest.

As mentioned before, this chakra has a connection with the water element, and with good reason. When you think of water, you think of something that is fluid, adaptable, and constantly changing. This is a good way to think of the energy of the Sacral Chakra. Your creative energy is centered in this chakra.

When the Sacral Chakra is balanced, you'll enjoy the pleasurable aspects of life, such as sexual pleasure, without overindulging on them. You'll feel a sense of fulfillment from your creative pursuits and focus on happiness and pleasure. You'll also feel a deeper connection to the world around you through your emotions.

Someone with a Sacral Chakra that is balanced will often go with the flow. Change is easy for them, and doesn't present any undue hardship. They'll enjoy food and sexuality but not overindulge.

However, when the Sacral Chakra is blocked or deficient, you may feel sluggish, uninspired or numb. You may experience a lower sex drive as a result of this, or have a hard time achieving satisfaction in your sex life. You may feel stuck in a particular emotion, or mood. Conversely, if you have an overactive Sacral

Chakra, you may overindulge in fantasies, emotions, or pleasure, including sexual obsession. Either way, an imbalance in the Sacral Chakra causes you to be ruled by your emotions, instead of controlling them.

A balanced Sacral Chakra allows you to lead a healthy emotional life, providing a good basis to reaching the higher chakras.

## Navel Chakra

The Navel Chakra, or "Manipura," is located, as its name indicates, at the navel center. It is the third chakra in the list of seven and the last of the "lower," or more material, chakras.

This chakra is represented by an upside-down triangle in a yellow flower with 10 petals, and is frequently associated with the color yellow. It is also associated with the element of fire, and the inner fire inside us from which we draw power.

This chakra houses the energy for our personal power, the force of will that drives us forward in our lives and gives us momentum. From this chakra comes your sense of self-confidence and empowerment. It serves the function of honing your personal power to go through your life with confidence, determination and strength.

Its location near the digestive system is quite important. The is the chakra associated with the process by which your body turns matter into energy. Similarly, the Navel Chakra helps you digest your life experiences, using them as fuel for your self-confidence.

Momentum is the key word with the Navel Chakra. This chakra provides you with the power to move forward, to take your ambitions and intentions and make them a reality. It also governs your direction in life, and can influence your self-perception.

The Navel Chakra has a connection with fire for a number of reasons. The consuming nature of fire relates to your body's metabolism, which breaks down food into energy for you. The Navel Chakra governs these metabolic processes. In addition, the Navel Chakra provides you with the energy for strength and self-determination, like a burning flame.

When the Navel Chakra is balanced, you'll feel confident, steadfast, and empowered in your decisions and in the direction of your life. You'll feel a greater sense of purpose in your life, beginning to understand who you are and why you are here, and you'll begin to let go of the material things that you have begun to overvalue. It also helps bring you into balance in your relationships with others.

However, when this chakra is out of balance, you may begin to feel weak, guilty, or experience low self-esteem. If this chakra is deficient or blocked, you may begin to feel less assured in yourself, experience feelings of helplessness and irresponsibility, and have trouble making decisions. This can hinder your ability for self-expression, or lead you to make plans without realizing efficient ways to execute them. If this chakra is overactive, however, you may feel angry and ill-tempered, aggressive or controlling.

This is the last of the lower three chakras, focusing on your body and your earthly aspirations. From here on out, we begin to move to the more spiritual chakras.

## Heart Chakra

The Heart Chakra, or "Anahata," is found at the heart's center. It is the fourth chakra on our list of seven.

This chakra is represented by a six-pointed star in a green flower with 10 petals, and has a connection with the color green. It is aligned with the element of air, symbolizing its emotional qualities such as love and openness.

This chakra is the center for love, compassion, and kindness within us. The energy within this chakra empowers these highly positive attributes, promoting love for others as well as love for yourself. It also helps you tap into a sense of unconditional love, as well as connecting you to other properties of the higher self.

The heart chakra is the bridge between the three lower, more earthly chakras, and the three higher, more spiritual chakras. It has connections to both, governing love in all its facets, both helping you choose love in your day-to-day interactions and guiding you in your connection to a more all-encompassing, unconditional love.

The heart chakra is also associated with healing. This is the chakra that helps you with transformation and change, helping you grieve and reach peace. It also helps you down the path to forgiveness and acceptance.

Air, the fourth element, has a connection with this chakra. Its energy is very fluid, associated with the breath and its movements. This chakra is filled with movement and the capacity for change. This also relates to the idea of connection with all things through breath and air, which relates to the compassionate side of this chakra.

When you're able to balance this chakra, you'll be able to choose compassion and love, even in situations where it's difficult. You'll be a loving person, sharing compassion with yourself and others equally. A balanced Heart Chakra will allow you to feel connected with the world around you, and give you a deep appreciation of beauty.

However, when the Heart Chakra is imbalanced, you may feel difficulties with your emotions or with relating to others. If this chakra is overactive, you may put others too far before yourself and sacrifice too much of your own well-being for the love of another. If this chakra is blocked or underactive, however, you may feel like there is a wall around you, blocking love and positive emotions. You may find it hard to relate, empathize, or connect with family, friends, and those around you.

Now, we move onto the three higher chakras. These chakras are more spiritual in nature, and relate more closely to your search for enlightenment and truth.

## Throat Chakra

The Throat Chakra, or "Vishuddha," is found at the base of the throat. It is the fifth chakra on our list of seven.

This chakra is represented by a downward-facing triangle in a blue flower with 16 petals, and has a connection with the color blue. It is aligned with the element of aether, or space, which relates to this chakra's role in allowing you to project your voice into the world. It also serves as your connection to your etheric body, which is said to be the perfect template, or blueprint, for the other dimensions of your body.

The Throat Chakra is focused on your personal voice and your capacity for self-expression. It is this chakra that governs the energy for you to communicate and project your ideas and your truth into the world.

You may understand much of your self-truth already, but it is a different matter to be able to express that truth with confidence and conviction. That is where this chakra comes in. The Throat Chakra allows you to speak your truth clearly and compassionately.

This chakra not only allows you to speak your inner truth, however, but live it with conviction. It has a natural connection with the second chakra, the Sacral Chakra, which has a similar connection to creativity. While the Sacral Chakra is the wellspring for your creativity, the Throat Chakra allows you to express and project your creativity out into the world in an authentic manner.

This chakra has a connection with the element of aether, or space. This chakra connects you with your etheric body. You can think of that as the first layer in your aura, which connects to both your physical body and to higher entities.

When the Throat Chakra is in balance, you'll feel confident to share your inner truth and wisdom, enlightening and enriching the lives of those around you. You'll feel outgoing and able to connect with others. You'll also feel a sense of purpose and validation in your chosen path.

However, when this chakra is no longer balanced, you may begin to have issues with your communication. If your chakra is overactive, you may talk over others and keep others from sharing their truth. It could also lead to you talking too much, or being aggressive and mean in your interpersonal conversations. A blocked Throat Chakra may leave you feeling timid and unable to express your thoughts around others. It can lead to introversion and a sense of insecurity.

## Third Eye Chakra

The Third Eye Chakra, or "Ajna," is found between the eyebrows. It is the sixth chakra on our list of seven.

This chakra is represented by a two-petaled lotus flower, and has a connection with the color indigo. It is not associated with any element, as at this point this chakra is considered beyond the physical elements. Instead, it is associated with the "supreme element," all the elements together in their purest form.

This chakra is your beacon for enlightenment, allowing you to tune into the physical world and the world of spiritual energy. It is the seat of the conscious and unconscious mind, and is associated with perception, psychic energy, and intuition.

This chakra marks the beginning of an entry to the spiritual world, freeing you from the nature of time-bound consciousness.

For that reason, this chakra is very important and significant in our study of spiritual healing. We'll go over it in-depth later.

For now, though, what you need to know is that the third eye allows you to perceive energy beyond the physical world, achieving a connection with higher senses. It is also associated with your consciousness, especially altered states of consciousness.

As a result, when you awaken your third eye, you begin to experience a different way of sight and perception. It allows you access into the world of the intangible. These visions are hard to describe and require a much different approach than balancing the chakras we've mentioned previously.

Aside from its metaphysical properties, the Third Eye Chakra is associated with inner knowledge and self-assurance. It not only allows you greater insight into the world around you but also to yourself.

It's very rare to have an overactive Third Eye Chakra, as it takes concentration, diligence, and focus to achieve that sort of connection. It's much more likely that you have a blocked Third Eye Chakra. This results in you disregarding your connection to the spiritual world and the higher planes, only focusing on the material world. It can also result in you being unable to see the bigger picture in your life, focusing instead on the daily grind and your problems that result from that. It can also interfere with your ability to set a vision for yourself.

# Crown Chakra

Now we reach the end of the list! The Crown Chakra, or "Sahasrara," is found at the top of the head. It is the seventh and final chakra.

This chakra is represented by a many-petalled purple lotus, and is associated with the color purple. It is not associated with a physical element, as like the Third Eye Chakra is is considered to be beyond the elements.

The Crown Chakra connects your consciousness to the consciousness of the entire universe. It gives you access to the higher states of consciousness in the universe as you grow beyond your personal preconceptions and beliefs. You can think of the Crown Chakra as a door into these higher states of being.

It is this chakra that gives you access to wisdom and all else that is sacred. It allows you to commune with higher states of consciousness, leaving behind the bounds of space and time.

When immersed in the energy of the Crown Chakra, you will feel a sense of union with the universe -- a quite blissful ecstasy. It is in this state that you will receive the utmost clarity and wisdom.

Needless to say, this is not very common. In fact, it is quite difficult to achieve balance in this chakra. It is the pursuit of this enlightenment that often leads to an enriching and beautiful life, even if that enlightenment is never achieved.

This chakra is different from the others in that there really is no set method to balancing it. Instead, you should focus on achieving balance in the other chakras in your body; only when all are aligned is the path to enlightenment made clear.

Now, we have an understanding of the seven chakras making up the nexus of energy that flows through your body. The next step is understanding how to unblock inactive chakras. From there, we'll move into chakra meditation, the uses of each chakra, and how to achieve total balance, before moving on to the secret techniques for opening your third eye.

Remember -- above all else, enjoy these techniques! They are designed to make you feel freer and happier. There is a justification for why so many people have tried to reach enlightenment and healing for their lives -- it's the most fun practice you can have. If you think things chakras, healing, and spirituality are dark and depressing, then you're misunderstanding their purpose. The most aware masters are people who laugh a lot and enjoy life. Let's make sure our journey is a fun one!

# Chapter 3 Exercise to activate your chakras

By this point you have probably heard of yoga, at least a few times, and have seen it or practiced it on your own. You may also know people, friends and colleagues who talk about their yoga practice that they go to twice a week and how great it has been for their health and vitality.

These texts were the source of many religious, spiritual and cultural practice and are continuing to be practiced today.

These practices have also made their debuts in other countries and cultures and today, Yoga is one of the most practiced forms of physical fitness and wellness-care in Western culture, as well as where it originated from. It has become a regular institution of the modern world and has been known for centuries for its healing benefits and ability to increase life span, encourage healthy muscles, bones and tissues, and help the practitioner enter a transcendent state of calm through the use of postures, breathing techniques, and meditation.

The world of yoga is vast and there are a variety of practices, beliefs and techniques that have been developed by various gurus, bringing more knowledge and identity to each type of yoga and the purpose of those practices. There are dozens of different styles of yoga, and here are the yoga practices that are most commonly practiced in the West today:

Hatha Yoga- This is a broad term to incorporate a lot of different postures and poses that are often used in a variety of other yoga practices. The purpose of this style is to bring about more strength and physical vitality through better breath and posture. All of the poses are strength-building, or tend to be, and will be complimented by soothing stretch.

Ashtanga Yoga- This style of yoga is much more physically demanding and is useful for a more advanced practitioner. The word Ashtanga translates to mean "eight-limb path" and is a very vigorous compliment to some of the more gentle and rebalancing yoga styles.

Vinyasa Yoga- This, like Ashtanga, is a more advanced, quicker-paced and athletic form of yoga. It builds of the rigorous work of Ashtanga and makes for an even more challenging body work out. The outcome is to create greater flexibility, more powerful breath and deeper alignment with the whole being. The word Vinyasa translates to mean "to place in a special way."

Iyengar Yoga- These poses are precise, slow, and involve a lot of breath control. This practice is meant to aid in alignment. There are very small adjustments made and usually props, like bolsters or stretching bands, will be utilized to perfect form and posture. It is a much more calming and deeply relaxing workout.

Bikram Yoga- This style of yoga has become a sensation because it uses heat to help your body release toxins and work in a warmer room setting for optimum purging and cleansing. It would be like doing yoga in a sauna, usually at around 105 degrees F.

Yin Yoga- Yin is the word to describe the divine feminine energy in each of us. Like the Iyengar practice, it is slow and relaxing and tends to be seated a majority of the time. In this practice, poses are held for much longer periods of time to allow for a deeper stretch. It is meant for healing, inner peace and relaxation.

Jivamukti Yoga- Based on the Vinyasa practice, this style incorporates a great deal more chanting and spiritual teaching and guidance. It has more to do with being one with the Earth and everyone in it. You could say it is the exercise for opening the crown chakra.

Kundalini Yoga- This style of yoga is best known for awakening the Kundalini energy at the base of the spine that will lead to a full chakra rebalancing and awakening journey to enlightenment. It is often called "the yoga of awareness". You might say that this is the yoga for the chakras to heal, however they are all capable of keeping your energy centers cleansed and clear. Kundalini is based on the dormant energy being sparked to life and so all of the poses are intended to wake your "snake" and bring all of your chakras into alignment.

All of these yoga styles can be a beneficial to your chakra healing work. As you read through them and got a sense of what they might be best for, as far as physical health is concerned, you may also have gotten an idea of which chakra they can be easily correlated with. Even though they will have a general purging and rebalancing effect, while working on a specific chakra, you might be more inclined to go for a certain style.

For example, if you are trying to invigorate your energy and heal the blocks in your solar plexus, your right to act and your personal power, then you might want to go for the Ashtanga or the Vinyasa style. If you are trying to be more open in your heart chakra, the Yin yoga poses and rhythm might be a better choice, while the Jivamukti style can be beneficial to exercising your openness to the Universal light in everyone and in all places on Earth.

Even if you are interested in doing only yoga poses that are in alignment with a specific chakra energy, you can build upon your overall physical, emotional, spiritual, and energetic strength by practices any one of these yoga styles.

For some, the idea of going to the Kundalini practice makes the most sense when working on healing the chakras. The term Kundalini refers to the "coiled-up" energy at the base of your spine, where your root chakra sits, and the idea behind this yoga is that you will practice opening that dormant life-force energy to heal the whole chakra system. It can take many years of practice to go through it like this and it is worth it in addition to a couple of other practices that will help you enhance your journey so that you can get there a little faster.

The best way to decide what style of yoga works for you and your chakra healing practices is to try a few different styles and see what makes you feel the most aligned and one with yourself. You can view some samples of these styles on line through instructional videos, or you can try some classes at the local yoga studio. There are yoga teachers and yoga studios in every city and town these days, and so it won't be hard to find this healing practice.

Even if you are feeling stuck in your chakra awakening and rebalancing, yoga can help you to reorganize your energy and get back on track, so that you feel better equipped and supported to continue your healing journey.

# Chapter 4 The meditation process

Meditation and visualization are the basic steps of chakra balancing. It is imperative to understand that chakras are not physical areas. They are the centers where the concentration of some kind of energy is higher than the rest of your body. Abnormal concentration of energy in one place can cause problems. However, there is no way to move this energy physically as these chakras are not present inside your spine. They are outside your spine or alongside your spine. Physical manipulation of this energy isn't possible. However, this energy can be moved through focus. This is where meditation and visualization come into play.

Meditation helps you in bringing your focus to a point and move the energy from one part to another. This energy is directly connected to our subconscious. Our awareness can help in moving the energies into the required areas. You can carry out complete exchange and transition through meditation and visualization.

We are talking of two terms here: meditation and visualization. It is important that you understand the significance and role of both the processes.

# Meditation

Meditation is a broader process. It is a technique that helps in gathering your life energies and putting them to optimal use. Meditation can enable you to hold an iron-fist focus that can divert and streamline energies.

For most people, meditation is another way to de-stress. They believe that it is a fancy technique to reduce mind chatter. These are mostly western concepts. In eastern traditions, meditation is the ultimate way to establish a connection with the higher consciousness. Meditation helps you in looking inward, beyond the boundaries of physical perception. The ancient knowledge of the east that is getting so much appreciation today is a result of meditative practices.

Meditation can play a very important role in healing the chakras. It empowers your mind to actually locate the point of the problem and channel the energies to that point for healing. From opening the closed chakra to healing to activate the blocked chakra, everything is possible through meditation. There are several ways to deal with chakras, but meditation is one of the best ways to do so.

# Visualization

Visualization is a sub-process of meditation. It is an additional part that can help you in reaching the meditative state faster. It helps the people who don't have the practice of sitting quietly for long hours and thinking in an organized and focused way by guiding them.

Too much involvement of gadgets and technology in life, excessive influence of TV, and other audio-visual stimuli and other such things have made life harder for our mind. To add salt to the injury, we are living life at a breakneck speed. This compels most of us to have to multi-task many things in order to catch up with the speed of our peers. All this eventually leads to clouding up of the mind. We are constantly thinking all the time. Our mind is never at peace. This isn't the end of our worries.

Another big curse of this modern lifestyle is decision-fatigue. We have so many options in everything that we are constantly making a choice. This may look like a boon, but it isn't so for our brain. You stand in front of the mirror in the morning and find yourself confused about which shirt to wear. It is not the shortage of commodity but its abundance that has led to this problem of choice. We have made a boon a big bane for our mind. The choice would leave us dissatisfied. We would keep pondering about not picking up the other one. This would begin the chain of miseries for us. This question isn't important, and it wouldn't have any significance in our lives, but it would keep our mind engaged. It would keep weighing it down. From choosing between tea and coffee to choosing a life partner and from minuscule to magnificent, we are making such decisions every day for all our lives. This makes our brain foggy and tired. It gets into a habit of remaining engaged. It is never silent or straight. It is always making strategies and counterstrategies, even when they are not required.

This can make the simple process of closing the eyes and not thinking of anything near impossible. If you have ever tried to do this, you'll know that it is a lot more difficult task than it sounds. As soon as there is silence, our mind starts racing in all directions, and the continuous chatter makes focusing near impossible.

As soon as we close our eyes, another thing that happens is that our mind starts magnifying or accentuating our fears. It is the right time to generate the fight or flight response for perceived threats on which you might have to make decisions in fear. The mind starts bringing them in front of you. This can scare many people. It also starts running a painful past in the quick flashback as a refresher course to keep you trained and tamed. These are some of the steps the brain takes to keep itself engaged and maintain the habit of constant work.

Majority of people encounter this problem and are never able to really focus. They are never able to achieve the meditative state where they can harness the energy of the chakras.

Visualization is a medium with which you can keep the mind engaged and guide it to the desired point. It is an additional tool in meditation to help you reach the meditative state.

As you close your eyes, a sound in the background will guide you throughout the process to think about some specific things. Your mind would remain engaged and follow the orders. This trains it to think in a positive direction. Slowly and gradually, you can learn to meditate even without the help of visualization and would be able to get better results.

Meditation and visualization together can help you in making the mind chatter inconsequential. They will help you in raising your consciousness levels above your body and guide the energy points. It is a great way to open, activate, balance, and heal the chakras.

Meditation is a complete process. It doesn't require anything or anyone else once you have become trained in it. It is the only path that can be followed for awakening the crown chakra, too. Spirituality and meditation are the only two things combined that can help you in blossoming 'Sahasrara.'

With the help of meditation, you will be able to keep your mind at peace. The mental chatter is not a real problem. Our mind is equipped to several things at a time. It keeps thinking even when you are fast asleep. However, when this chatter starts interfering with your conscious decisions, then it becomes a real problem. If there would be too much mental chatter, your mind would get cluttered. It would lose its sharpness. It would get dull and unresponsive. That will prove to be a problem in your personal, professional, and spiritual upliftment.

With the help of meditation, you can train your mind to ignore this chatter. You will also be able to develop better power of discernment. You will be able to distinguish facts from fiction. You will not get confused between real and imaginary. You will know the difference between truth and myth. All these things will help in clearing the clutter. You will be able to think more clearly. Your mind would feel more energized and focused.

Meditation is the means, and the practice of visualization is a helping tool.

When you use both of these things for chakra balancing, you will be able to get faster results. The risk of failures and disappointments decrease.

Chakra balancing becomes a very simple task once your focus is streamlined. You simply need to sit still and put your focus on the problem areas. Slowly and gradually, you will have to try to pull or push that energy upward or downward as needed.

## The Ways to Do It

There are several ways to meditate. Every tradition has established several ways of meditation. Each way only aims a single thing, and that is building focus. There are several meditation techniques that have become very popular all around the globe.

Some of the popular meditation techniques are as follows.

## Breathing and Relaxation Meditation

This is a simple yet very effective meditation technique that allows you to develop deep focus by paying attention to your breath. The air that you breath travels to most vital organs on your spinal cord. This is the path on which the chakras are based, and the energies are working. You can help in moving the energies through this breathing meditation technique. It is very easy to follow,and you can perfect it over the course of time.

## Mindful Meditation

This is a meditation technique in which you start by creating awareness in your mind. In place of trying to regulate your mind, breath, or any other process, you simply become an observer and look at the genesis of thoughts in your mind causing the clutter. You get to the root of your fears. You learn the process of overcoming the challenges posed by the mind by facing them directly.

It starts by simple observation and then you can begin training your process of thoughts. This is one of the most effective meditation methods for people who suffer from fears, anxiety, and panic attacks. You learn the process of understanding the problem and then addressing it.

## Loving-Kindness Meditation

This is a meditation process that helps you in generating sweetness of emotions. It is a part of Buddhist meditation processes and helps a lot in curbing anger, temptation, guilt, frustration, and other such feelings. If you are full of negativity about the world and don't find it fit for your mercy, you should practice this meditation first before working on your chakras.

The chakras have a very delicate balance. They can get imbalanced at any kind of surge. If you start working on your chakras with such a mentality, it can harm you a lot. The chakras can increase these tendencies to a very dangerous level. You can start having mental issues.

Before managing the chakras, it is very important that you manage your mind first. Trying to harness the powers of chakras with a poor mental state can be very dangerous for yourself.

This is a wonderful meditation practice for such issues. It helps in addressing the internal issues and makes you more grateful to society. You are able to feel the contributions of others and also able to see the areas in which you have not been able to play your part properly. It brings humility to your heart and makes you a balanced and better person. With humility in heart, the chakras can help you in becoming a wonderful person.

## Mantra Meditation

This meditation practice comes from India. It uses certain mantras or recitals to raise the vibrations in your mind. The Sanskrit mantras help in touching specific energy waves which can help. Mantras for chakras are not complex ones but simple sounds. When you repeat them in sync, they cause reverberations. Even if you don't have the knowledge of Sanskrit, you can recite these mantras as they are mostly single-syllable words. If you start repeating them in continuity, they become simple sounds, and you can feel their reverberations inside you.

The process of this meditation is also the same. With a simple addition of certain sounds, you can begin the mantra meditation.

## Body Scan Meditation

This is an excellent meditation technique through which you develop the ability to touch various energy points in your body through your consciousness. It can help a lot in healing various chakras and restoring the balance.

If you don't have a feeling of wellness and are never satisfied with the way you are, this meditation technique can be the thing you need.

## Chakra Meditation

This is specifically a chakra awakening technique in which you learn the ways to harness the energies based on various chakras. This meditation will not only help you in restoring the energy balance, but it can also be used to open and activate closed chakras. While the lower chakras in our body are generally open and functioning, the upper three chakras remain dormant. You specifically need to follow various methods to activate those chakras. This meditation deals with those methods.

Chakra meditation requires great control and devotion. You would have to maintain certain specific postures so that proper focus can be put on the energy centers. Everything mentioned in this chakra is specifically pointed toward awakening of the higher chakras.

## Third Eye Meditation

Like chakra meditation, this is also toward activation and awakening of chakras. This chakra is specifically designed to help in activating the third eye chakra. People with an interest in gaining a higher sense of perception, psychic powers, and greater consciousness can follow this meditation.

This is a top-order chakra; hence, one should be very careful while activating this chakra. The true masters of this chakra stand testimony to the fact that it is not an easy chakra to navigate through. The intensity of this chakra is so high that it can leave even trained meditators frightened at times.

This chakra also uses colors, mantras, and specific positions for faster activation.

## Gazing Meditation

This is a simple meditation technique for all those people who find it very difficult to focus with the eyes closed. If your thoughts stray a lot or you get frightened due to darker thoughts, you can follow this meditation practice. As the name suggests, you will need to maintain focus at some point with your eyes open. The object of your attention could be a picture, dot, flame, point, or anything else. You will need to keep looking until your mind gets stable and then you can proceed by closing your eyes.

## Guided Meditation

Guided meditations are a great help for the people beginning their journey with meditation. The sounds guide you through the whole process. Your mind remains focused with the help of imagery described in the recitation, and it helps you in visualizing the right things. This process is especially very helpful if you have fear of going into deep focus, or you face problem in building focus.

## Zazen or Zen Meditation

This is a Buddhist meditation technique which focuses on the right posture and following the mindfulness as a way of life. This technique doesn't limit you to the right posture and breathing techniques only during the meditation sessions; it dictates that you have to be mindful in every step of life. Either you are cooking, playing, laughing, or taking a bath, you will have to remain mindful of everything. You can't do anything without putting your consciousness into it.

Zen mastery involves transforming life on a consciousness level. You become mindful of everything in life; hence, all desires, guilts, expectations, and regrets go away. It is the path of letting go of the unnecessary things in life.

These are some of the paths that can be followed in meditation. There are hundreds of more meditation techniques that are followed all across the globe. They may have difference in form or principle. However, one thing that's common in every technique is that they all focus on raising the level of consciousness to activate and regulate energies in the body.

## Position

Some meditation techniques lay great emphasis on the postures. They would ask you to sit in a full lotus position, while others may give you a bit of relaxation and allow half-lotus position. There are even some meditation techniques that may not require you to sit at all. You can get into a meditative state while lying down on the bed or walking. It is not the form that matters but the kind of focus you are able to build. If you can reach the center of your consciousness even while walking in the park, there can be nothing better than that. You must not fret about the method, but look if it is going to serve the ultimate purpose of the exercise.

## Time

It is one thing that may vary among various types of meditation techniques. However, the most important thing that matters is your ability to build the focus at the time of meditation.

The best time to begin meditation is early in the morning as positive energies are very high at that time. Your body is also well-rested; hence, it is able to summon the energies well. Another thing that can be avoided easily at this time is the burden of the day's negative influence. The whole day's functioning may have a great impact on the functioning of the mind; hence, it may take you longer to build focus at the end of the day.

However, meditation should also be done at the end of the day, as it helps in keeping the energies aligned. If you meditate at night before sleeping, your chakras are stimulated to radiate positive energy. It is especially good for your physical as well as mental health.

# Chapter 5 What are crystals

Crystals are considered "in-organic" by the scientific community. That may be true, but if you have ever held one in your hand, you may have noticed or sensed the energy emitting from the stone, and how alive it feels. Crystals and gemstones are formed inside of the Earth through intense pressure, water and other chemical compounds that help to "grow" these unique elements.

You have seen many ladies wearing diamond engagement rings, no doubt. All of these were formed under very intense pressure and conditions to form one of the most expensive gems around. They are cut in specific ways and set into rings in order to be worn by a bride to be, or someone who is displaying their love of something sparkling. Few people realize how powerful the energy emitted from a diamond actually is. It has a huge potential force of energy radiating off it, specifically because of how it was formed in the ground that it was mined from.

When you wear a diamond ring on your finger, or any other crystal or gemstone, your entire energy field is connecting to that same energy and aligning with that frequency. It can be so subtle that no one would really notice it, especially if it is a small jewel, but when you are dealing with the larger rocks and crystals, you can feel a more potent and powerful energy pushing out of it.

Since you have learned about the science of chakras and the frequency that they radiate, then you can understand why and how crystals, which do the same thing, would have the same effect. Like you, a crystal will absorb and contain energy inside of it and so when people use healing stones and crystals for their work, you will often find that they will use energy clearing methods on their own crystals!

Harmonic resonance is something that can occur between two energies that will synchronize their energy flow in order to be in harmony with one another. Think of a rock band that plays songs together: they play notes that harmonize together and are sticking to a particular rhythm or beat, in order to make a song. All of the musicians synchronize their energy in order to play a song from beginning to end. If they didn't have harmonic resonance, the song would be all over the place and wouldn't sound very musical at all.

With crystals, you can achieve harmonic resonance between your energy and the energy of the crystal in order to regain or rebalance your own frequencies. You can enjoy a new kind of inner rhythm when you bring a crystal or gemstone close to your heart chakra, worn as a necklace, or to your root chakra when carried in your pocket.

For several people who are interested in using crystals for chakra healing therapy, you can simply add it to your meditations and yoga practices by physically laying the stone on top of each chakra placement on the body while you lie on your back.

Lying in position for several minutes with a large piece of quartz crystal, or kyanite on your abdomen, will effectively shift and recharge the energy of your solar plexus so that you can begin to go through a greater purging and processing of the emotions or blocks stored there.

To be clear, crystals don't magically eliminate the issues you are holding onto. The way that they work is to magnify the energy that you are holding onto that needs to be released, bringing it to the surface so that you can let go of it fully.

Let's see an example of that: Let's say after about 30 minutes of meditation with a crystal placed on your heart chakra, you get up feeling refreshed, relaxed, calm and excited to feel an open heart and new lease on love and life. Later that night, you start to feel really sad and depressed and will even burst into tears out of nowhere. You are having thoughts about your last relationship pop up, even though you feel completely over that experience and have nothing further to do with it. You are even happy for your ex, that they got married and found the right partner for themselves. So why are you thinking about your relationship and while feeling sad out of nowhere?

The answer is that as soon as you stopped using the crystal therapy in your afternoon meditation, your whole energy system began to shift and re-coordinate and after several hours of feeling like everything was going to work out just fine, you suddenly felt tragically sad. Your heart chakra was showing you exactly what was still blocking your ability to open up to a new lover, or partner. Even though you thought you were over it, you still had a residual energetic feeling of sorrow.

After recognizing this, let's say you do some journaling about that time in your life and you get to the part where your ex is happy and in love and a newly wed while you are still struggling to find the right partnership for yourself. You discover that you have feelings of happiness for your ex, however you are feeling a longing for what they have and a sense of not knowing if it will ever happen for you the way it happened for them.

All of this because you put a crystal on your heart chakra and meditated. Here's the thing though: if you are going to use crystals for chakra healing, don't expect a profound healing discovery every time you use one. It doesn't always work that way and it can take a lot of time and practice to effectively read the signals of your energy in order to interpret what is slapping you in the face to be healed and released.

Don't get discouraged if you don't have any big epiphanies or breakthroughs right off the bat. You can have a lot of other very profound, healing experiences when you work with crystals and they do have a powerful energetic impact on your whole energy system when regularly used, or even only used sporadically.

Because ever type of crystal has its own energy frequency, there are some that are more effective for certain chakras than others and the following list will be helpful for you, if you are not familiar with crystals and gemstones, to locate the right one for your healing needs:

Root chakra: Black Tourmaline, Bloodstone, Carnelian, Garnet, Hematite, Tiger's Eye, Fiery Agate, Red Jasper, Smoky Quartz, Black Kyanite, Obsidian

Sacral Chakra: Amber, Aragonite, Citrine, Carnelian, Orange Coral, Moonstone, Orange Aventurine, Orange Calcite, Red Jasper, Snowflake Obsidian,

Solar Plexus: Citrine, Calcite, Yellow Tourmaline, Lemon Quartz, Sunstone, Peridot, Topaz, Malachite, Quartz Crystal, Amber, Yellow Jasper

Heart Chakra: Green Calcite, Emerald, Jade, Rose Quartz, Rhodochrosite, Rhodonite, Green Tourmaline, Green Aventurine, Amazonite

Throat Chakra: Turquoise, Angelite, Aquamarine, Celestite Crystal, Lapis Lazuli, Blue Calcite, Blue Amazonite, Blue Apatite, Scolecite,

Brow Chakra: Quartz Crystal, Purple Fluorite, Labradorite, Shungite, Amethyst, Azurite, Black Obsidian, Sodalite

Crown Chakra: Quartz Crystal, Diamond, Kyanite, Lepidolite, Selenite, Sugilite, Amethyst, Charoite, White Calcite

All of these stones are intended for each chakra to create a harmonic resonance that will leave you feeling awakened and aware, as well as to help you kick start some purging and cleansing of your chakra energy blockages. There are so many stones that are not on this list that will also be helpful in your healing experience. The best way to choose a stone for yourself is to hold it in your hand and see how well you resonate with that energy.

Some people feel that certain crystals and gemstones will "call" to them and have exactly the right energy that they need right then. Since your energy is never constant and always shifting and rebalancing, the kind of stone that you need will change from time to time as well. It can be useful to have a few to choose from and having a selection for healing purposes is a great goal to have.

There is another stone that is often used as a Universal chakra healing stone that has an ability to stay fully charged at its own frequency without needing to be cleansed of absorbed energy: Blue Kyanite.

This stone, since it does not collect negative vibrations, is a cleansing tool for other stones and crystals, as well as for your own chakra energy. In fact, it is known as the chakra healing stone as it has the power to help you align all of your chakras. This can be a great choice for a beginner to use since it will work well for every chakra as well as for the whole system of energy.

Using Blue Kyanite regularly during healing meditations and crystal healing work will show you how to effectively shift and alter your energy with one, simple piece of the Earth's treasures.

So, how do you heal yourself with crystals? As mentioned, you can simply lay them over each chakra as you meditate and there are a few other ways that you can use them to keep yourself in balance and focused on your healing:

Wear them as jewelry everywhere you go, or carry them in your pocket.

Add them to your bath water when you have a relaxing soak in the tub.

Place them under your pillow to enjoy restful, healing sleep.

Add them to your drinking water and let them infuse the water with healing vibration for you to drink.

Put them in your shoes overnight so your feet will feel empowered while you walk around all day long.

Rest them on the skin of your face to give you a youthful glow and vibrant skin.

Plant them in the vegetable garden in your yard to infuse the soil and the food growing in it with high vibrational energy.

Place them in a circle around your yoga mat so that they are beaming high vibrations to you while you work on your flexibility and strength.

These are just a few possibilities and you are likely to stumble across a few more in your daily life. The applications are endless! You will also need to keep your stones energetically "pure" for regular use. If they are absorbing negative energies and vibrations, then you will need to make sure that they are properly cleansed after using them a few times during healing meditations.

Here are some basic ways to keep your crystals and gemstones cleansed and free of unwanted vibrational energies:

Place them in warm salt water for half an hour.

Set them outside in the sun for several hours.

Place them next to, or on top of, a piece of Blue Kyanite.

Smudge them with incense (ancient purifying technique using smoke).

Try some of these methods to keep your crystals fresh and clean, ready for healing use.

In order to get the best benefit from healing with crystals, here is a general meditation that you can use on any chakra with a corresponding crystal or gemstone:

General Guidelines for Chakra Healing with Crystals:

Lie in a comfortable position on the floor, or on a bed or other surface.

Place the stone on the desired chakra.

Take several deep, relaxing breaths and connect to your body.

Through your breathing, connect to the energy of the stone. Concentrate on feeling its energy.

Allow yourself feel your own energy connecting to the stone. Pay close attention and continue breathing deeply and slowly.

Focus on your feelings in this area. What ideas/thoughts/images/memories are coming up for you here?

Spend time "listening" to your energy and allow it to surface as needed. Experience the energy of its manifestation and let it flow into the stone resting on your chakra.

Picture the negative ideas/thoughts/memories/images being released into the stone and leaving your body.

Visualize your chakra being recharged and bright in light. Feel the energy of this stone taking hold of your wounds and pain and relieving you of them.

Remove the stone from your chakra and meditate on how your energy feels. Allow yourself to process any deeper feelings and emotions that might have surfaced. Be prepared for thoughts and feelings to surface later on, after you are done meditating.

These basic instructions are all you need to get you started with healing with crystals. You can apply these basic steps to every chakra and it will take as little as 10 minutes to as long as an hour. You are going to find a lot of healing energy from these little Earth treasures, and the more you use them, the better you will heal. They can be quite impressive in their abilities and will really help you magnify the issues that need unblocking. Consider using them in every chakra meditation you do to get you started on your healing path.

Moving forward into the next section, you will learn what Yoga is and how it has an impact on your chakra energy.

# Chapter 6 The Power of Crystals

Traditional Indian medicine defines chakras as a concept of wheel-like vortices that are placed on ethereal doubles of mankind. Chakras are seen as centers of energy, and in these centers, energy unfolds and gains shape pinpointed in the physical body. These rotating vortexes of energetic matter are believed to be receptors and transmitters of energy. There are many chakra systems but the one that is used most is the system of seven chakras. Chakras in this system are seen in a flower-like shape where a predetermined number of "petals" that are shown in a circle-like shape is divided into segments and each chakra has its own number of them.

Chakras represent important points of energy, and we can use them consciously or unconsciously. These points allow us to understand the things that are happening around us. These important points named chakras are placed on crucial parts of our body such as our head or heart, for example. It is believed that through chakras, a person can control their mind and bodily activities. As it was already explained, humans possess seven chakras, and they can be found aligned with the spinal cord. Each chakra has its own characteristics, and they all influence different nerve plexuses. Chakras correlate to all sorts of energy bodies and they have the task of absorbing a life force called Prana, and then distribute it to the physical body.

The Root Chakra (Muladhara)

The first chakra is called the root chakra or Muladhara. It is symbolized as a four petal lotus and it is located at the bottom of the spine. It is said that Muldhara controls physical energy and that it helps with everyday activities and survival. Muladhara is called the root chakra because it represents the foundation and it is a kind of transcendental basis for one's own physical nature. Additionally, this chakra is known as the seat of the 'red bindu', which will rise up to the 'white bindu' in the head to unify male and female energies of the gods Shakti and Shiva. Muldhara is connected to the sense of smell and it is the element of earth. It is believed that the person who concentrates on the root chakra through meditation can develop various powers such as becoming free of disease.

The Sacral Chakra (Svadhishana)

The second chakra is called Swadhisthana and it is portrayed as a six petal lotus. This chakra can be found slightly below the navel, and it is the chakra that is in charge of emotional energy. The second chakra is connected with the subconsciousness and with feelings. It is very close to the first chakra, but in Swadhisthana the potential karma of the person can be found dormant. On the other hand, this potential karma finds expression in the first chakra. Swadhisthana is connected to reproduction and the sense of taste. It is also associated with water as its main element. This second chakra is associated with one's unconscious desires, and it is said that his chakra enhances the energy of consciousness. Since it is the energetic center for emotions and desires, activating Swadhisthana is considered to be very difficult. The person who meditates on this chakra can be freed from their enemies, and they can improve in speaking and reasoning.

The Solar Plexus Chakra (Manipura)

The third chakra is called Manipura and is portrayed as a ten-petal lotus. This chakra is located at the solar plexus of the individual and it has the role of controlling the astral energies. This chakra is considered to be the chakra of willpower and one's connection to the world of dreams. The tradition of Vajrayana explains the importance of the navel wheel due to the fact that it is the seat of the 'red drop'. This 'drop' refers to red-colored triangles that have 64 petals, or in this case, channels that are extended upwards. Meditation based on the syllable "Ah" is the main practice component of inner fire meditation called Tummo. With Tummo, energy enters into the central channel, travels up to the top, and causes a feeling of bliss. This kind of meditation and these types of practices are one of the most important yoga foundations.

The Heart Chakra (Anahata)

The next chakra is the heart chakra, or otherwise called - the Anahata. It is portrayed as a twelve-petal lotus and it can be found on the heart. This chakra is important because it controls mental energy. Anahata is described as the chakra of compassion and love, and it is said that this chakra portrays the Buddha's nature and Dharmakayan posture. Upanishads (a series of sacred Hindu treatises) describe Anahata as a small flame that is placed inside one's heart. The name Anahata (sound without striking of objects) originates from the fact that sages were believed to have been able to hear sound from the place where the chakra is positioned. The main element of this chakra is air, and it influences sense of touch and anything connected to the hands. The heart chakra is described as the chakra that enables a person to make a decision without considering karma. It is important to keep in mind that Manipura and chakras below, are all bound by the karmic laws of karma, but with the heart chakra, one's decisions are based on following one's heart and one's instincts. This is a chakra that associates people with feelings of compassion and charity, and it is good for physical healing. If a person meditates on the heart chakra it will bring powers that are considered to be occult. If the one meditating is a man, he can become more attractive to females.

The Throat Chakra (Vishudda)

The fifth chakra is the Vishuddha Chakra, denoted by a sixteen petal lotus. This chakra can be found on the throat and it is in charge of one's spiritual energy. This chakra is important because it is closely related to a person's expression and creativity. The fifth chakra is also the purification center, and it divides energies into pure and impure ones. Vishuddha is associated with the power of self-expression and with one's creativity. When a person closes or blocks the fifth chakra, decay and even death might be inevitable, because if opened, this chakra takes all negative experiences of the person and transforms it into a lesson learned. The throat chakra is so important that even the failure or success of the person is determined by the condition of this chakra in one's body. The main element for Vishuddha is ether, and it is connected to the sense of hearing and the power of speech. If one is meditating on the fifth chakra it can obtain so-called occult powers such as visions of the past, visions of the present and visions of the future. It can also have the ability to weave through these three worlds.

The Third Eye Chakra (Ajna)

The Third Eye Chakra is the sixth chakra that is also called Ajna, and it is portrayed as the ninety-six petal lotus. This chakra can be found between the eyes, or precisely in the center of the forehead. This area is also known as the "Third Eye". The sixth chakra controls cosmic energy and it is the chakra of so-called higher knowledge and deepened perception. The term Ajna means 'command' and it is the name given to this chakra because the third eye is considered to be the sense for intuition. Someone could see something in their dreams, and believe it has been seen by its Ajna or their third eye. Hindu people have a belief that spiritual energy that enters the body goes through this chakra, and that Ajna is a kind of shield from bad influences of other energies - this is why Hindu people mark the foreheads of men and women. According to them, it is a blessing and demonstration of respect to their gods. If a person meditates and concentrates on the Third Eye Chakra they can also obtain these so-called occult powers such as entering other bodies and becoming omniscient.

The Crown Chakra (Sahasrara)

The final chakra, the seventh, is known as the Crown Chakra or Sahasrara. This chakra is portrayed as a thousand petal lotus and it is situated on the crown of one's head. This chakra rules with Nirvanic energy and it is believed to be the chakra of high spiritual consciousness. The seventh chakra enables detachment from illusion for the person, and it represents the basic element for gaining higher consciousness. It helps the person realize the truth behind the premise "one is all and all is one". This chakra is usually referred to as Sahasrara, and it is believed that this is the most subtle chakra of the seven. It is connected to pure consciousness, and from here, all other chakras emanate. When a person who practices energy shifts levels its energy up to the state of Samādhi, it is said that the person will feel indescribable bliss. Meditation while focusing on the seventh chakra can give powers such as divine transformation.

## The 7 Layers of Human Auras

The aura consists of three sections. The first one is the innermost section; the second one is the inner section, and the third one is called the midsection. The section that is the easiest to see is the inner section of an aura, while the innermost section is portrayed as white, thin light. Additionally, the midsection of an aura reflects a person's emotions, wellbeing, and health along with their personality traits. Even though there are many theories on the aura's layers, the most common one is the theory that divides auras into seven layers. The names can be slightly different for some layers in other texts, but they are all recognizable.

Each layer has a different meaning. The first one is the one that is closest to the person's body called the physical layer. Going onward from the physical layer, there is the ethereal layer, then the vital layer, the layer connected to the astral plane, a layer of lower mental state, a higher mental layer, and finally the spiritual layer. As previously explained, these layers can have slightly different names in the literature. The role of the physical layer is that it emits the physical needs of the person, especially the ones connected to their comfort and health. The second layer is one that represents emotions and feelings. The third layer focuses on desires and thoughts, and state of mind. The astral (fourth) layer centers around one's desire for love from their family, friends, or partner. The lower mental (fifth) layer is associated with balancing spiritual energy and desire for the truth; two things that need to be harmonized. The higher mental (sixth) layer is one that is focused on acquiring happiness and spiritual love. And finally, the spiritual (seventh) layer is one that is connected to the divine. It is a layer that helps the person understand higher forms of things and feelings.

There are cultures that connect aura layers directly to the chakras. The Kundalini tradition, for example, has its first aura layer, the ethereal one, associated with the root chakra; their second aura layer is the emotional one and it is connected to the sacral chakra; the mental body layer is connected to the solar plexus chakra; the astral one is associated with the heart chakra; the fifth chakra is connected to the esoteric template; the sixth chakra is related to the celestial layer; and last but not least is the crown chakra, related to the causal body layer.

# Chapter 7 The Healing Benefits of Crystals and Stones

Cleansing our chakras will help bring them back into balance but sometimes there is no blockage or negative energy in the chakra. It may be that a chakra is just very weak, sluggish or in some cases it could even be over active.

The following carefully chosen crystals and crystal healing methods will help bring all your chakras back into balance.

## Crystals that Balance all the Chakras:

Turquoise

Usable Forms: Tumble Stone, Unpolished Crystal

Description: This stone ranges from sky blue to blue green. It can have darker veins or some mottling with brown or white. Genuine Turquoise is much sought after and has been mined for thousands of years.

Balancing Properties: This is a gentle healing crystal that balances your energy on many levels. Turquoise slows down over active chakras and brings sluggish chakras back into a healthy balance again.

Fluorite

Usable Forms: Tumble Stone, Unpolished Crystal, Crystal Wand

Description: This magical crystal comes in a variety of clear colours. It is often banded or a mixture of colours. Fluorite can be clear, purple, blue, green, yellow and white. For Chakra Balancing purposes look for a mixture of at least two colours or more. The mixed Fluorite is sometimes called Rainbow Fluorite.

Balancing Properties: When Fluorite is placed within the chakras it quickly works to bring the energies back into balance and harmony with each other. Fluorite also balances all the layers of the aura.

Ammolite

Usable Forms: Polished Crystal, Unpolished Crystal

Description: Also known as Opalized Ammonite. This is an Ammonite fossil that has gleaming bright colours caused by mineralization over thousands of years. Ammolite was once an ancient sea creature, but is now a gemstone.

Balancing Properties: Ammolite plugs you into the Universal life force that harmonises and balances your aura. It spiritually attunes each Chakra to its optimum frequency and colour vibration.

## Quartz Crystal with a Rainbow

Usable Forms: Tumble Stone, Crystal Point, Crystal Wand

Description: This feature is caused by a natural internal flaw within a clear Quartz crystal that produces a rainbow colour effect. It is only noticeable when the flaw catches the light at the right angle so always check your crystals for rainbows!

Balancing Properties: This type of clear Quartz specialises in balancing the chakras and all the layers of the aura. These crystals work on many levels and very quickly bring your energies back into a healthy balance again.

## Gaia Stone

Usable Forms: Polished Stone

Description: Gaia Stone is created with the ash from a volcanic eruption at Mount St Helens in the USA. This man made gemstone is similar in composition to Obsidian, a volcanic glass. Gaia Stone is clear and has a deep emerald green colour.

Balancing Properties: Gaia Stone harmonises you with the natural order and energies of the Earth. Its healing emerald green rays bring balance to the energy centres, balancing all the Chakras in a gentle way.

## Angel Aura

Usable Forms: Tumble Stone, Crystal Point

Description: Also known as Opal Aura. This is Quartz crystal, which has been bonded with precious metals such as Silver and Titanium. This creates a clear coated crystal with iridescent pastel rainbow colours.

Cleansing Properties: This ethereal crystal tunes and balances all the chakras with its rainbow energy. It banishes lower energies and also clears the chakras with its high vibration angelic light.

Spectrolite

Usable Forms: Tumble Stone, Polished Stone

Description: Genuine Spectrolite is a unique variety of Labradorite only found in Finland. It is black with intense and metallic colours, which shift and shine when it catches the light. Unlike common grey Labradorite it can be found in all colours of the spectrum.

Balancing Properties: Mystical Spectrolite sends beams of multicoloured light deep into the chakras. It tunes the chakra to a balanced but higher vibration. This stone works to align the chakras with the Earth and the greater Universe.

## Ways to Use a Single Crystal to Balance all the Chakras

Wearing or carrying any of these harmonious crystals will help keep your chakras balanced. The most effective method to use these crystals is to put them directly in the chakras or use them in meditation.

As always if you do not wish to include the Soul Star or Earth Star Chakras in any of these methods you can just skip to the next chakra.

# How to Balance Your Chakras with a Single Tumble Stone (Laying Down)

As with selecting crystals for a Chakra Crystal Set make sure your crystal has at least one flat side so that it can be laid on the body securely. If the crystal you have does not come as a Tumble Stone use a polished or unpolished stone.

Find a quiet comfortable place to lie down.

Place your crystal about 6" below your feet within the location of the Earth Star Chakra.

Lay down facing up and get into a comfortable position. Take a few deep breaths.

Close your eyes and visualise yourself as being a large strong tree with roots going deep into the Earth.

See your roots reaching the very centre of the Earth where they wrap around a large Iron crystal.

Sit up and move the crystal to your Root Chaka location. Lay back and relax for a about a minute or longer if you prefer.

Then move the crystal up to the Sacral Chakra. Continue up the chakras leaving the crystal on each chakra for about a minute.

Lastly place the crystal about 6" above the top of your head for the Soul Star Chakra.

Open your eyes and take a few moments before getting up again.

## How to Balance Your Chakras with a Single Tumble Stone (Sitting)

Similar to the method above but you will have to use your arms in this one. With practice this will become easier like a Yoga pose.

Sit down with your legs crossed or on a chair and take a few deep breaths.

Place your crystal on the floor either between your legs or under the chair. This is for the Earth Star Chakra.

Visualise yourself as being a large strong tree with roots going deep into the Earth.

See your roots reaching the very centre of the Earth where they wrap around a large Iron crystal.

Next with both hands hold your crystal in the position of your Root Chakra. Close your eyes and hold it there for about a minute or longer if you wish.

Continue raising the crystal up through all the Major Chakras. Spending about a minute with each one.

For the Soul Star Chakra you will have to hold it with both hands about 6" above the head. Your arms will form a circular shape.

Once finished put the crystal down safely. Raise your arms and shake them out.

Open your eyes and take a few moments before getting up again.

# How to Balance Your Chakras with a Crystal Point or Wand

Working on yourself with a Crystal Point or Crystal Wand is more involved than using a Chakra Crystal Set. You may of course get a like-minded friend to use the crystal on your chakras.

Sit down with your legs crossed or on a chair while holding your crystal in your dominant hand.

Close your eyes and take a few deep breaths.

Visualise yourself as being a large strong tree with roots going deep into the Earth.

See your roots reaching the very centre of the Earth where they wrap around a large Iron crystal.

Open your eyes, lower your hand and point your crystal down towards the floor to the location of the Earth Star Chakra somewhere below your feet.

In a small clockwise circular motion direct your crystal towards this chakra for about one minute or longer if you wish.

Next move to the Root Chakra, You can point the crystal inwards now towards this area and again use circular motions for about a minute.

Continue up through all the Major Chakras, balancing them one by one. For the Crown Chakra you can point the crystal downward towards the top of your head.

For the Soul Star Chakra point the crystal upwards, just above the top of your head directing it in a circular motion as before. Take a few moments before getting up again.

## How to Balance Your Chakras with a Single Crystal in Meditation

You can use any form of chakra balancing crystal. With a natural Crystal Point or Crystal Wand, have the crystal pointing upwards in your hands.

Sit down with your legs crossed or on a chair and close your eyes.

Hold your crystal in your hands on your lap and take a few deep breaths.

Visualise yourself as being a large strong tree with roots going deep into the Earth.

See your roots reaching the very centre of the Earth where they wrap around a large Iron crystal.

Focus on the crystal you are holding and visualise it begin to glow with light.

Visualise a luminous ball of soft white light descending onto your Soul Star Chakra. For about a minute see this ball of light surrounding this chakra.

Now see the ball of light moving down onto the Crown Chakra. Repeat this process down through all the chakras. Spending about a minute with each one.

Lastly visualise the ball of light descending down into the centre of the Earth.

Open your eyes and take a few moments before getting up again.

9 – Chakra Hacks: Crystals That Align All The Chakras

When your chakras are aligned they will be all lined up with each other. Your chakras system will be fully connected to the centre of the Earth, the greater Universe and your higher self. This allows for the greater flow of divine energy and wisdom to come through you.

Chakra alignment can help you feel more connected, present and better able to handle anything that comes your way. This is something you may wish to do after you have cleared and balanced your chakras.

The following selection of crystals and crystal healing methods will align and connect all your chakras.

## Crystals that Align all the Chakras:

## Boji Stones

Usable Forms: Unpolished crystals

Description: Genuine Boji Stones come with a yellow certificate. They are small earthy rough and heavy disc shaped stones. They normally come as balanced pairs, one male and one female. Boji Stones also have an unusual magnetic polarity.

Aligning Properties: Through their polarised energy signature Boji Stones draw your energy towards your core and anchor it like a magnetic iron bar.

## Faden Quartz

Usable Forms: Unpolished Crystal

Description: These are flat double terminated clear Quartz crystals. Inside the crystals is a single ribbon like white band that runs horizontally through the centre of the crystal.

Aligning Properties: Soothing Faden Quartz brings all the chakras back into alignment. It connects the Chakra System to the Earth's core and the centre of the Galaxy.

## Black Tourmaline

Usable Forms: Crystal Point, Tumble Stone

Description: Tourmaline grows into long crystal points usually with three sides. If left unpolished it will have grooves or striations on the sides. Black Tourmaline is jet black and opaque.

Aligning Properties: Black Tourmaline allows for the free flow of energy up and down the chakras. This stone firmly anchors your aura and energy body with the Earth's natural energy field.

Spectrolite

Usable Forms: Tumble Stone, Polished Stone

Description: Genuine Spectrolite is a unique variety of Labradorite only found in Finland. It is black with intense and metallic colours, which shift and shine when it catches the light. Unlike common grey Labradorite it can be found in all colours of the spectrum.

Aligning Properties: Spectrolite anchors the light emanating from the chakras and realigns it with your spiritual core, Earth and the Galaxy. Spectrolite also balances the chakras.

## Chrysanthemum Stone

Usable Forms: Tumble Stone, Polished Stone

Description: These black stones have a white flower like pattern. They look like flower fossils but the star burst pattern is actually formed by crystal formations within the stone.

Aligning Properties: Chrysanthemum Stone is deeply grounding. It draws your energy down into the heart of the Earth. Aligning your chakras with the body and skeletal system.

## Ways to Use Crystals to Align all the Chakras

Wearing or carrying these crystals will help keep your chakras aligned. The most effective method to use these crystals is to put them directly into the chakras or use them in meditation.

Please note that you can use a single crystal or a pair of the same crystals for chakra alignment. Boji Stones for example come in pairs but you could also use a pair of Chrysanthemum Stones if you wish. When working with pairs of crystals follow the instructions below but have one crystal in each hand.

## Working with Chakra Crystal Sets

You can also use any of the chakra aligning crystals in this chapter for the position of the Earth Star Chakra in a Chakra Crystal Set.

The other way is to hold a pair of the chakra aligning crystals while you're doing chakra balancing and clearing with a Chakra Crystal Set. These methods are ideal when you do not know what is most needed or want to cleanse, balance and align all your chakras in one session.

## How to Align Your Chakras with Crystals (Laying Down)

As with selecting crystals for a Chakra Crystal Set make sure your crystal has at least one flat side so that it can be laid on the body securely. If the crystal you have does not come as a Tumble Stone use a polished or unpolished crystal.

Find a quiet comfortable place to lie down.

Place your crystal or crystals about 6" below your feet within the location of the Earth Star Chakra.

Lay down facing up and get into a comfortable position. Take a few deep breaths.

Close your eyes and visualise yourself as being a large strong tree with roots going deep into the Earth.

See your roots reaching the very centre of the Earth where they wrap around a large Iron crystal.

Sit up and move the crystal to your Root Chaka location. Lay back for a few seconds.

Now slowly move the crystal up to the Sacral Chakra. Continue up the chakras pausing only for a few seconds.

Lastly move the crystal about 6" above the top of your head for the Soul Star Chakra.

Open your eyes and take a few moments before getting up again.

## How to Align Your Chakras with Crystals (Sitting)

Similar to the method above but you will have to use your arms a little with this one.

Sit down with your legs crossed or on a chair and take a few deep breaths.

Place your crystal or crystals on the floor either between your legs or under the chair. This is for the Earth Star Chakra.

Visualise yourself as being a large strong tree with roots going deep into the Earth.

See your roots reaching the very centre of the Earth where they wrap around a large Iron crystal.

Next with both hands hold your crystal in the position of your Root Chakra. Pause for a few seconds.

Continue raising the crystal up through all the Major Chakras. Spending just a few seconds at each point.

For the Soul Star Chakra you will have to hold it with both hands about 6" above the head. Your arms will form a circular shape.

Once finished put the crystal down safely. Raise your arms and shake them out.

Open your eyes and take a few moments before getting up again.

## How to Align Your Chakras with Crystals in Meditation

Sit down with your legs crossed or on a chair and close your eyes.

Hold your crystal or pair of crystals in your hands on your lap and take a few deep breaths.

Visualise yourself as being a large strong tree with roots going deep into the Earth.

See your roots reaching the very centre of the Earth where they wrap around a large Iron crystal.

Focus on the crystal you are holding and visualise it begin to glow with light.

Visualise a beam of white light projecting downwards from your crystal towards the centre of the Earth.

Now see a beam of light shining upwards from your crystal through all your chakras up into the sky.

Lastly visualise this pillar of white light and feel your chakras aligning.

When this feels complete, open your eyes and take a few moments before getting up again.

# Chapter 8 Ways to Align the Chakras Beyond Meditation

In addition to meditation, there are plenty of other methods that you can seek out that will help to release and activate your chakra energies within. This chapter is going to look at what you can do when you're already meditating and still would like to open your chakras in other ways. After reading this chapter, you will have many options when you're looking to open up any of your chakra energy centers. As you're going to see, many of these techniques are able to target the chakras in different ways. This means that not only

will you have options when it comes to opening your chakras; you will also have variety in terms of how you're going about doing it.

Using Reiki to Align the Chakras

Reiki is a practice that's used to reduce stress in individuals and promotes optimal relaxation. When you attend a

Reiki session, you are going to lay on a table, similar to how you would when you're getting a massage. Taken apart, the "Rei" in Reiki can be translated to mean "wisdom from a higher power

," while the "Ki" can be translated to mean "life force" or "eternal energy." In other words, the point of Reiki is for the Reiki therapist to guide the energy of the individual towards greater harmony and alignment with the rest of the body. As you can see, Reiki has been known to directly influence the way in which chakra energy flows in the body.

When you're participating in a Reiki session, the therapist is not going to touch your physical body. Instead, you are going to close your eyes, and the instructor is going to place his or her hands

on top of your main chakra points. These subtle placements of the hands over the body is able to positively influence the energy within. Many Reiki participants walk away from Reiki feeling revitalized, happier, and far more relaxed than when they first entered the

healing room.

Using Aromatherapy to Align the Chakras

In addition to treating yourself to Reiki, another way that you can align your chakras is through aromatherapy techniques. In opposition to Reiki, aromatherapy emphasizes the physical placement of essential oils on the chakra centers of the body, in an attempt to reach the chakra topically. You can perform aromatherapy on yourself by simply rubbing a drop or two of an essential oil of your choosing over the area of the body where the chakra energy is located. Below you will find a list of essential oils that can be used when you're looking to target a specific chakra area of the body:

| Chakra | Best Essential Oils |
|---|---|
| Root Chakra | Patchouli oil or rosewood oil |
| Sacral Chakra | Jasmine oil or sandalwood oil |
| Solar Plexus Chakra | Peppermint oil or cedarwood oil |
| Heart Chakra | Cypress oil or geranium oil |
| Third Eye Chakra | Lavender oil or marjoram oil |
| Crown Chakra | Myrrh oil or helichrysum oil |

Using Crystal Healing to Align the Chakras

If Reiki and aromatherapy do not seem like chakra aligning avenues that you're interested in taking, you still have the option of aligning the chakras through crystal healing. Crystal healing is all about surrounding yourself with the color that is associated with the chakra that you're trying to open. We've already discussed the colors that are associated with each chakra along the length of the spine. When your eyes frequently see the color related to a certain chakra energy center, they're able to bring this stimulus to the energy that surrounds that chakra. Perhaps more significant, colors also have frequencies of light that travel along a wavelength.

When you use crystals as a way to balance the chakras, these wavelengths of energy are able to transcend the visual stimulus from the eyes and penetrate into the chakra in question. You can purchase

crystal stones rather cheaply, although there are one out there that are on the more expensive side. Another technique that could be useful is to first surround yourself with the particular chakra color that you're trying to embody. Next, find a place where you can comfortably meditate. Next, meditate on the color that you've chosen. With the crystals around you and your mind focused on that color, you will be able to tap into the energies with

in your subtle body.

Using Yoga to Align the Chakras

Lastly, developing a yoga practice that focuses on the seven chakras is a fabulous way to get in touch with energy that is unbalanced or needs some awakening. Generally speaking, any yoga pose that requires sitting down is going to be good for the root chakra. This includes stretching. When you're trying to focus on any chakra point in relation to yoga, you're going to want to make sure that you're paying attention to doing poses that will utilize the spine in that specific chakra energy center whenever possible. You could also link certain poses together and create a flow for yourself that targets each chakra to some degree. Seek out yoga classes in your area that perhaps emphasize chakra healing. If you find a class like this, don't be afraid to ask the instructor questions regarding chakra balancing. He or she will likely have even more techniques that you can try out.

In conjunction with a chakra yoga practice, chanting is also a great way to target a specific chakra in the body. Chanting can be done at either the beginning or the end of a yoga session.

OM, in particular, is a chant that can cause the body to feel complete and elation and bliss when spoken or sang. Another way to incorporate chants into your yoga or meditation practice is a mantra. A mantra is a phrase or group of words that

are typically chanted in Sanskrit. Mantras can range from simple to

complex and are known to be able to invite the spirits of the Hindu gods and goddesses into an individual's vicinity. Even if you don't believe in the Hindu gods and goddesses, chanting can still be a form of sound therapy for the body. OM is just one example of the many mantras that you can chant either on your own or in a group as a way to generate greater chakra abilities.

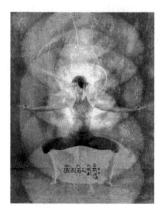

# Chapter 9 The Healing Process

It is very difficult to change habits. They are formed with continuous revisions and hence, become our second nature. However, the problem with habits is that they are simply not guiding our behavior; they also make it very difficult to change the problematic ones.

When there is an imbalance in a chakra or some chakra is lacking in energy, you don't get a knee-jerk reaction all of a sudden. It's not like someone has suddenly applied brakes on a car doing 100 mph. When there is a problem in a chakra, you start exhibiting behavior that would prevent you from taking corrective action.

For instance, if the energies in your root chakra go out of balance, you can start losing your ground. You may start making imaginary castles and avoid doing any kind of groundwork.

The first part of the problem is to identify it. Once you know that there is a certain problematic behavior, you must understand the reason behind it. If the problem is in the root chakra, you will have to take remedial steps in all possible directions. You may use crystals. You should do meditation for better grounding. Yoga will help you in correcting the problem. But, even if you do all this and you physically correct the problem, practically, the things would remain the same for you.

Habits form over time, and they tend to stick if you don't put conscious effort in correcting them. You would have to improve your habits in any condition.

If you start correcting the habits even before you have begun the corrective measures, bringing the balance would get much easier.

When you are trying to change a habit, you put conscious effort into it. You become mindful of your energies and your tendencies. Suppose there is a problem in the solar plexus chakra, and you have started shirking from work. Even if the energies get balanced, you will have to bring yourself back to work. The work wouldn't come walking to you. Your energies will only return by balancing the chakra; the tendencies have to be developed through practice and developing positive habits.

## The Ways to Do It

## Become Conscious of Your Decisions

The best way to change habits is to become conscious of your decision-making process. Our mind has a very sophisticated fight or flight response system. It will always present two ways to approach a problem, and you pick the easiest one with least confrontation as a default. However, if you are conscious of your decisions, you can avoid choosing the easy way that inevitably is the tough way. You can avoid confrontations temporarily, but that approach never ends the problem. But, you can only do this when you are conscious of your decision-making process.

You will have to critically analyze things in your life and then decide if the step is going to be good for you or not.

## Be Mindful in Your Actions

Always remain mindful of the actions you take; changing a habit is not easy. Habits make us do things instinctively. A person habitual of using reading glasses may squint the eyes even after the need for glasses has ceased to exist. It is a reflex action that has developed over time. It is not very easy and pleasant to remind oneself of avoiding this every time. However, in some situations, it is very important.

Being mindful helps in getting out of the trap of such habits and practices. Your mind can not only avoid repeating such actions, but it will not initiate them in the first place.

## Why Does It Work

When you change your old habits, you are reminding yourself that you are ready to accept the new change. It increases your readiness and also makes you more receptive. This fills your body with positivity. The chakras react favorably to the flow of positive energy in any desired section. Hence, the process of bringing the balance becomes easier.

You must understand that energies are fluid. They would be able to penetrate and flow easily in the area which has a positive reception.

As you become more mindful of the chakra where there is an imbalance, it also helps in opening up the chakra. Your focus on that chakra will give it a positive impetus.

## Advantages and Disadvantages of Using This Method

Advantages

It is a highly effective method.

It helps you in experiencing the change on a personal level.

This raises the level of optimism inside you.

Serious change begins, and you are at the driving seat of this change. This gives you the feeling that you have gained control. It is a very positive feeling.

Disadvantages

The process is tedious and highly repetitive.

It can look as if you are being asked to do a lot of work.

Habits are a great reflection of an individual's personality. Sometimes, people are too adamant, arrogant, and even unaware of their impact to other people and environment. The realization of the negative impacts of their habits is the hardest part for most people. Once you acknowledge the problem in some of your habits, don't be reluctant to change them.

Most people believe that once there is a change in the energy levels in their chakras, everything else will improve on its own. It may be true on a macro level. However, on a micro level, that change has to be felt by you. You are the person for whom the change is being brought. If your bad habits don't go away, you will not be able to get the real benefits of that change.

This is the first step that you can't miss, irrespective of the method you choose to bring changes in your energy levels.

# Chapter 10 Using Crystals For Reiki

Chakra blocking can have a very serious impact on your life. Each chakra in the body influences some vital organs. It is also responsible for regulating specific emotions inside you. If your chakras get blocked, all of these can get affected. You may start feeling your life going out of balance.

Some people wrongly believe that chakras are the source of energy, and if they keep working on improving the functioning of a specific chakra, their life will become easier. Nothing could be farther from the truth. Chakras are not the source of energy. They are simply the points where the life energy in your body manifests itself in a different way. They work like transformers.

The energy that is coming to these chakras is the same. The root chakra and the third eye chakra both have different roles in your body. They affect different parts of your body. But, the energy they are getting is the same. It is only the nature of the chakra that makes the energy work in a different way. If any of the chakras are blocked in your body, the overall flow of energy gets affected. The upper, as well as the lower chakras, stop getting a regular flow of energy. Some chakras start getting less energy while others start getting more, neither of which is good for you.

We have already discussed the impact of high and low energy on all the chakras in your body. All this can be prevented if you can prevent blockage of the chakras.

Blockage in chakras leads to psychological issues. There are specific symptoms of energy imbalance in any chakra. You will have to remain watchful of the psychological issues faced. Specific organs in your body also start getting affected. These are clear tell-tale signs that there are problems in your energy field. You will have to remain watchful of these symptoms to ensure that there is no blockage in your chakras.

Remember that all the chakras are a part of a system. They are working together as a unit while maintaining their individual function. If the blockage in one chakra is ignored, it will have a deep impact on other chakras too.

For instance, you will never be able to activate your third eye successfully if there is a blockage in your root chakra. The root chakra is responsible for keeping you grounded in reality. If you activate your third eye chakra while your root chakra is not balanced, you may become delusional. You will have no clear discernment between what is real or imaginary.

Although your higher chakras are blocked, the functioning of lower chakras will also get affected as your spiritual consciousness would be very low. You would become too much focused only on yourself. You may have no control over your intellectual powers.

Every chakra shows clear signs of blocking. You must understand the signs and work toward opening the closed chakras. You can also use various healing techniques for opening the blocked chakras.

The signs given below may serve the purpose of a ready reckoner in case you are actually having a blockage in any chakra.

## Root Chakra

Blockage in this chakra will make you fearful. You may have unreasonable concerns about safety and security. You may start having the fight or flight response very frequently. You would start losing the grounding effect, and you may become more dreamy and impractical. The feeling of being tied down and difficulty in letting your fears go away is also a common sign.

## Sacral Chakra

One of the first signs of this chakra being blocked is a diminishing sexual desire. You may start facing difficulties in experiencing joy. If you start getting hyper-emotional even over petty issues and face difficulties in adapting to changes, then it means that there are problems in this chakra. Becoming overly sexual and feeling guilty about it is also a common sign of a blockage in this chakra.

## Solar Plexus Chakra

If you have started losing confidence all of a sudden or have a feeling of low-esteem, this chakra can be blocked. This is the chakra of fulfilling desires. If you are facing problems in focusing on work or your over-reliance on others for success is increasing, this chakra can be blocked. Fatigue, allergies, indigestion, and hypertension are some of the signals of the problem in this chakra.

## Heart Chakra

If you have started feeling too lonely all of a sudden, or you are having frequent problems in relationships, then this chakra can be blocked. Lack of emotional fulfillment and difficulty in giving or receiving love is a specific indication of problems in this chakra. Feeling of disconnection with nature or divine force or unresolved sorrows are also an indication of the blocked heart chakra.

## Throat Chakra

Communication problems are a clear indicator that this chakra is not functioning properly. If you are having any problem in conveying ideas, expressions, problems, or creative mediums, then it may indicate that the throat chakra is not functioning normally.

## Third Eye Chakra

Blockage in the third eye chakra may lead to a lack of imagination, perception, and vision. Your power of intuition would get cluttered. You may also face problems in looking at the big picture while conceptualizing things. If you have started becoming delusional or your imagination has got distorted, then this is also an indication that your third eye chakra is blocked.

# Crown Chakra

Blockage in this chakra may make you impractical and indecisive. You may have problems finishing things you started, and you may start feeling depressed, alienated, and confused. There may be an unexplained restlessness in your mind that keeps you agitated. A sense of meaningless and loss of purpose in life are strong signals that your crown chakra is blocked.

In case you are observing the symptoms mentioned above, you must consult an energy healer. An energy healer would be able to find the exact chakra blocked in your body. You can use the chakra healing techniques mentioned in the following chapters to heal your chakras and open the blocked chakras.

Chakras are energy centers in our body that are running on a very delicate balance. Your psychological, emotional, and physical state can have a deep impact on the functioning of the chakras in your body. In the same way, your chakras can also have a profound impact on these factors. There is a cause of every imbalance, and there is an effect of every kind of action. It is important to know the cause and effect your steps can have on treating the problem.

Chakra imbalance or blockage is not a permanent phenomenon. You can easily open the blocked chakras and activate the chakras which are closed. You can also balance the chakras that have excessive or deficient energy. All you need is the right technique and determination. This book will give you all the techniques needed for correcting the problems in every chakra.

# Chapter 11 Chakra Healing Techniques

Knowledge of chakra has not come out of thin air. It is a concept that our ancestors had been using for thousands of years to keep themselves happy, healthy, and balanced. They had understood the importance of a balanced life. They lived a much more content life even with their limited means than what we are leading today. From physical activity to a balanced diet, everything had its place in their lives. These are the things that we are missing these days, and it is causing a lot of problems in the balance of the chakras.

These days, our lives are so rigidly tied around gadgets that we have become overly dependent on them. In a way, machines have started running our lives. This has taken away our natural rhythm. We have started running after material wealth with so much conviction that we easily ignore physical, mental, and emotional boundaries. We remain indulged in competition in the rat race to a fictional success. This puts a lot of psychological, emotional, and physical pressure. This eventually trips the delicate balance of the chakras.

Chakra healing techniques don't require something monumental to be done. You would simply need to make some simple changes to your lifestyle. You would have to devote some time to physical activities like yoga or exercise so that the chakras can be stimulated physically. Meditation and visualization techniques can help in the stimulation of the chakras on the energy level. Crystals and essential oils can be used as tools to help your efforts in stimulating the chakras. All these things, in conjunction with each other, can help in the activation, healing, and balancing of the chakras easily.

These days life has become very chaotic. There is a lot of emotional turbulence. We have become emotionally volatile. We get agitated over simple things and find it very hard to bear even slight turbulence in our emotional state. All that is happening is because we have stopped working on our energies.

People find it very hard to remaining committed in relationships. They feel that relationships become very demanding with the passage of time. People find it really difficult to accommodate others in their personal space. Some people simply don't understand boundaries. All these issues are not new. Humankind has always been living in a society. Yet, these problems have become so severe all of a sudden. The prime reason for these problems is our inability to handle our emotions. We keep feeling crushed under the guilt of these failures. We try to find the solution to these problems in drugs, alcohol, and ways that can divert our mind momentarily. However, we all know that such solutions are temporary and don't last more than a few hours. In fact, they are a problem in themselves, as they lead to addictions and deterioration of health.

The challenges we face with other people are a reflection of imbalance inside our body. If the chakras in our body are balanced, such issues would never arise in the first place. You'd know the secret in remaining content, so others wouldn't have that kind of control over you. They wouldn't have the power to emotionally drag you down to such low points.

The chakra healing techniques will help you in bringing that balance back. You will learn simple chakra healing ways, through which you can restore chakra balance.

Here are some important ways to heal your chakras are:

Change of habits

Life balance

Creating your recharge center

Meditation and visualization

Yoga

Essential oils

Crystals

## Change Old Habits

Balancing the chakras is a holistic process. The chakra balance can get affected by many things. However, serious chakra imbalance is not a sudden change. It usually happens at a very slow pace. Our habits are symptoms, as well as reasons for serious chakra imbalance.

When there is some chakra imbalance in our body, it gets manifested as a certain trait. For instance, if your root chakra gets out of balance, you may start feeling ungrounded. You might start to have unreasonable fears. You might also start having frequent fight or flight response within you. This usually doesn't happen when your root chakra is functioning smoothly. A balanced root chakra ensures that you are a reasonable person. You will be able to assess the gravity of the situation quite reasonably.

However, root chakra can get out of balance due to several reasons, and most of the imbalances are temporary. It means that your chakras are constantly trying to maintain the balance. It is like a stream of a river. It always tries to make way irrespective of the diversions it gets. However, poor habits can work like dams. They might obstruct the flow of the river to a great extent. This is what may cause greater problems.

Suppose you become fearful of something; it is not uncommon for us to become afraid. Normally, that fear dissipates after some time. The body absorbs the shock. It gets over the incident and becomes normal. However, some people give that fear a permanent residence in their mind. They keep thinking about that incident only. This habit can come in the way of smooth flow of energy in the root chakra. Our chakras are also affected by our psychological and emotional state. When we make something our second nature, it seriously affects the functioning of the chakras in our body.

Serious imbalance in the chakras is always of our own making. Our habits and lifestyle affect the functioning of the chakras in a big way. If you want your chakras to work smoothly, you will have to inculcate good habits that support it.

From physical problems to emotional issues, everything is directly or indirectly connected to the imbalance in your chakras.

Let us take the example of weight gain. People who are overweight have one of the biggest challenges in their heart, and that is to lose weight. They are so burdened with the idea that their whole life starts revolving around this idea.

No doubt, weight loss is important as it affects your health in many ways. However, the feeling of failure of not being able to lose weight is even more harmful. People keep trying one method after the other to lose weight. It becomes the single most important pursuit in their lives. This is what gives way to chakra imbalance.

Weight gain can happen due to several reasons. Most of the times, when we have pain, suppression, unfulfilled desires, and fantasies at the back of our mind, which we can't fulfill, our mind starts overcompensating for the pain. The second chakra known as the sacral chakra goes into overdrive. You become a complete pleasure-seeker giving in to material pleasures. This gives way to addictions. We all know additions are tough, and they go away very painfully.

Imbalance in the sacral chakra will have a deep impact on your root chakra, as well as your solar plexus chakra. You will not only gain more weight, but you will also start losing the ability to lose weight in the future become your ways would become your habit.

The solution would have been to give an outlet to your suppressed emotions, to find an outlet for your problems. However, the mind tries to choose an easy way first to get rid of the pain momentarily, and that's fine, but to get addicted to it is dangerous.

We generally make comforting things our habit without thinking about the long-term repercussions they can have on our lives. Such things become a habit and keep damaging our chakra balance.

The best way to avoid chakra damage so we can heal the chakra imbalance is to inculcate healthy habits. You must identify the bad habits in your life and weed them out, one by one. Habits are a part of our lifestyle, and we adopt them as our second nature. We become unmindful of them, so they have a great influence on our lives.

You should include a two-step approach to change your bad habits:

Make Decisions Consciously: You may think that the word decision itself has an element of consciousness involved. Unfortunately, it doesn't pan out like that. We leave most of the crucial decisions in our life on our mood. We like things to be pleasant at the moment, and this paves the way to addictions. We don't make strong decisions. We don't act consciously as we are not even thinking consciously. Your first step should be to stop living in an autopilot mode and move to the driver's seat. Look at your life and the direction it is heading. Don't make the flight response a natural reaction to all the problems in life.

This will burden the chakras which are weak, and they may get blocked as other chakras will start acting dominantly. Critically analyze the problems in your life, and try to find the reasons behind them. Once you have derived a conclusion, take decisions to mend your ways. Most importantly, get out of the trap of bad habits.

Become Mindful: One of the biggest drawbacks of habits is that it doesn't require you to take decisions mindfully. Your body starts functioning in the autopilot mode, and there is a very small scope of active decision making. It is important that you become mindful of your habits and take decisions on merit and not on habit. Don't go by your innate response, but try to challenge the norms set by your habits. This will helps in changing the flow of energy in your body. It will stimulate the chakras which have been dormant.

Changing old habits may only be a small change in life, but it is a very big change in energy and experiential level. Your body starts to exhibit readiness for change, and the flow of energy starts correcting itself positively. You become more optimistic, and even your emotional state starts to change.

Remember, monumental changes don't come from knee-jerk reactions but from small and steady corrections that alter the fundamental functioning of the system.

## Journaling

You have done excellent work to get to this stage of Chakra Work—congratulate yourself! In this chapter we will discuss journaling your successes. Take time now to write down all the changes that have taken place in the last few weeks or months while doing the chakra work. Be sure to include how these changes have affected you and those around you. With practice, one day soon, you will read this detailed account of the changes that have taken place in your life to find that you are amazed at the changes.

The written documentation of you journey is very useful and important. It can serve as proof of how far you have come and how useful chakra work has been for you.

A few suggestions to make your journal more informative:

Each time you journal include the date.

Write down the changes you notice and the reason you came to notice them.

Include how you would have handled the same situation in the past, for example, in the past you might have been prone to depression that lasted a long time -- now, you notice that you are able to pull yourself out of it in only a short while.

Mention personal incidents to document the event or situation that has changed.

Write what other people have to say about the changes in you.

Note any resistance you get from others – sometimes those around us don't want to see us change and sometimes they simply cannot see the changes in us due to their own blocks and imbalances; other times they do not want us to get healthy because they fear they might also have to change.

Document any changes that have helped you at work, home, or community, for example if you have noticed that now you are more outgoing or assertive; more friendly with coworkers or family note this in your journal.

Note if the changes that are taking place in you are mental, physical, or spiritual, for example, if you have noticed that you have more mental clarity or if you have become more physically active – be sure to document it.

Document any diet changes, for example, if you have noticed any changes in cravings for certain foods or a sudden interest in being more health conscious.

Note any mood changes, for example, if you have noticed that you now wake up feeling rested and happy; more even tempered and relaxed; or that you find that you enjoy life more.

Mention any personal habits that have changed, for ex- ample if you have noticed that certain places, people, and activities are less appealing to you than they were before you started this spiritual work.

Other personal habits might pertain to your work or living space, be sure to note if you have noticed any improvements.

Note any feelings of satisfaction or dissatisfaction – any emotional feelings that might have changed from doing this work.

I know as you progress through the chakra work that you will attain your highest good. It simply works that way. And, as you do, I wish you the very best as you continue on this path of enlightenment.

# Chapter 12 Crystals For Chakra Balancing

The Root Chakra

When you are meditating on your root chakra, it is best to use one or several stones. Here's a list to help you choose a particular healing crystal to guide you on achieving a balanced root chakra: Black Obsidian, Red Zincite, Smoky Quartz, Hematite, Garnet Spinel, Zircon, and Black Tourmaline. All of these represent stability, physical energy, grounding, security, and will; characteristics associated with the root chakra.

The Sacral Chakra

When you are meditating on your sacral chakra, it is best to use one or several stones. Here's a list to help you choose a particular healing crystal to guide you on achieving a balanced sacral chakra: Vanadinite, Carnelian, Blue-green Fluorite, Copper, Imperial Topaz, Blue-green Turquoise, and Orange Calcite. All of these represent sexuality, reproduction, emotion, desire, creativity, and intuition; characteristics associated with the sacral chakra.

The Solar Plexus Chakra

When you are meditating on your solar plexus chakra, it is best to use one or several stones. Here's a list to help you choose a particular healing crystal to guide you on achieving a balanced solar plexus chakra: Gold Tigereye, Yellow Apatite, Golden Calcite, Yellow Jasper, Amber, and Citrine. All of these represent protection or one's protectiveness, personal power, intellect, and ambition; characteristics associated with the solar plexus chakra.

## The Heart Chakra

When you are meditating on your heart chakra, it is best to use one or several stones. Here's a list to help you choose a particular healing crystal to guide you on achieving a balanced heart chakra: Rose Quartz, Jade, Green Aventurine, Lepidolite, Rosasite, Pink or Rubellite Tourmaline, Cobaltian Calcite, Vesuvianite, Watermelon Tourmaline, Malachite, and Pink Danburite. All of these represent emotional balance, universal consciousness, compassion, and love; characteristics associated with the heart chakra.

## The Throat Chakra

When you are meditating on your throat chakra, it is best to use one or several stones. Here's a list to help you choose a particular healing crystal to guide you on achieving a balanced throat chakra: Blue Kyanite Chrysocolla, Sodalite, Celestite, Blue Chalcedony, Angelite, Aquamarine, Blue Calcite, Blue Turquoise, and Amazonite. All of these represent diving guidance, expression, and communication center; characteristics associated with the throat chakra.

The Third Eye Chakra

When you are meditating on your third eye chakra, it is best to use one or several stones. Here's a list to help you choose a particular healing crystal to guide you on achieving a balanced third eye chakra: Tanzanite, Lapis Lazuli, and Azurite. All of these represent spiritual awareness, intuition, psychic power, and light; characteristics associated with the third eye chakra.

The Crown Chakra

When you are meditating on your crown chakra, it is best to use one or several stones. Here's a list to help you choose a particular healing crystal to guide you on achieving a balanced crown chakra: Selenite, Amethyst, WhiteTopaz, White Howlite, Apophyllite, Herkimer Diamond, White Danburite, White Calcite, White Hemimorphite, and Quartz Crystal. All of these represent enlightenment, energy, perfection, and cosmic consciousness; characteristics associated with the crown chakra.

## Food For Your Chakras

The Root Chakra

If you want to balance your root chakra, think of its corresponding color – red! Moreover, since this chakra is called the "root chakra," then you may have guessed that foods like garlic, onions, beets, radishes, parsnips, potatoes, and carrots should be on top of your grocery list. In addition, you can also add foods that are rich in protein like peanut butter, soy food items, tofu, beans, meats, and eggs. If you're going to eat meat, opt for lean meats. Also, the flavors that suit this chakra point are a pepper, paprika, chives, and cayenne.

The Sacral Chakra

Alluding to the sacral chakra, which is situated at the navel, it is constantly associated with the color of orange. Thus, you may want to eat foods that are orange in color. This chakra is also related to everything enthusiastic and innovative. A sound sacral chakra consistently helps control and equalize one's life. Opt for more organic products like coconut, mangos, melons, and strawberries. Indeed, even nectar and nuts are suggested for helping you with sacral chakra meditation. With respect to flavors, vanilla, sesame seeds, as well as cinnamon, help to support this chakra. Also, try to add to your grocery list, carrots, apricots, peaches, foods that are rich in Omega-3s, various kinds of nuts, salmon, flax, and walnuts.

The Solar Plexus Chakra

The solar plexus chakra tries to accomplish balance in confidence issues and instinctive aptitudes. Consume more grains like oats, rice, flaxseed, and sunflower seeds. If you are going to eat rice, opt for brown rice. Try to also accustom yourself to adding rye, beans, and spelt to your daily meals. Drink more milk; eat more cheese; consume more yogurt. Fennel, chamomile, cumin, mint, ginger, and turmeric can also help with healing the solar plexus chakra, as well as foods that can provide you with sustainable energy and crucial fiber.

## The Heart Chakra

Psychological mistreatment and shock can be harmful to the seat of affection, the heart chakra. Guarantee that this chakra is consistently balanced by consuming green and raw foods. Think organic! Help the healing procedure by nourishing this chakra point with greens like broccoli, cabbage, cauliflower, celery, spinach, dandelion greens, and kale. On another note, green teas additionally maintain this particular chakra in great condition and zest it up with cilantro, basil, or thyme.

## The Throat Chakra

To keep the throat chakra balanced, consume fluids like water, organic product juices, and homegrown teas. Teas are very good as they are considered as soothing and healing liquids, as well as lemon water and honey. Healing foods to be consumed are as follows: apples, plums, pears, and other foods that are equipped with antioxidants, vitamins, and sources of fiber.

## The Third Eye Chakra

Prominently known as Ajna, the third eye chakra is situated in the focal point of the head or temple. It's the seat of intelligence and understanding. It keeps things in context. Dull pale blue organic products like blueberries, blackberries, and raspberries aid in keeping this particular chakra focused. Even grape juice or wine, alongside flavors such as poppy seeds, are viewed as ideal for this particular chakra.

The Crown Chakra

This is an important chakra point as it opens up otherworldly correspondences with the universe. It's regularly drawn or portrayed as a lotus blossoming and opening itself up to the world. Incense and smirching herbs like juniper, frankincense, copal, myrrh, and sage are best used when you are meditating on this energy center. Also, detoxifying and fasting are activities said to be useful for the advancement of this chakra.

In the end, we would like to ensure that everything presented in this book should serve as your guide, but must not all must be strictly implemented. We couldn't stress this enough – when it comes to chakra meditation, you must allow yourself to feel comfortable with yourself and with what is happening around you. This is the only way you can be honest and truthful as to how you really feel. If you are more honest about the things in your life, you'll be able to see things clearly. A good example as to what we're talking about is your stance when meditation. Of course, the most basic stance is sitting down, but there are those who prefer standing up or lying down. Moreover, there are also certain rules mentioned in this book that needs to be followed, such as the need to start at the bottom – with the root chakra – going up to the crown chakra. Lastly, we would like to provide you with a final note that achieving mindful and holistic health will take time. However, it doesn't mean that you should easily give up if, for the first time you've experienced meditative practice, did not notice any change in you. Remember that the benefits of chakra meditation will be brought to you by the universe gradually. Consistently be aware of your surroundings and it may come up to you when you least expect it.

## HOW CRYSTAL GRIDS WORK

Crystal Grids may not be the most simple way to use crystals, but they can be very effective. This is the reason more and more people are working with them. Later on I will show you step by step how to make both simple and more complex grids for yourself and others. But first we are going to explore how and why these arrangements of crystals work.

Crystal Grids combine the energies and properties of specific crystals with the mechanics of other metaphysical systems. This is all done with the intention of creating a desired result. What this means is that the energy of the crystals is focused, directed and amplified when used within a Crystal Grid.

The building blocks of all Crystal Grids are the crystals themselves. So let's start with the essential part of all Crystal Grids before we explore the other aspects. Please note that throughout this book I refer to the words crystal and stone interchangeably to include any mineral or gemstone.

# Crystals & Crystal Healing

Crystals have long been used for their therapeutic, spiritual or healing properties. What we now call Crystal Healing or Crystal Therapy today is the development of these ideas and traditional beliefs in modern times.

From a scientific point of view, crystals contain various combinations of minerals and have their own electromagnetic field. When we look at most crystals close up under high magnification we see they have a crystalline structure, which is geometric. This exists at a microscopic level and repeats throughout the whole crystal. Some crystals grow into clearly geometric formations such as Quartz, Amethyst, Pyrite and Fluorite to name but a few.

These fascinating geometries, energy fields, repeating patterns and structures all seem to add weight to the metaphysical belief that crystals emit and store energies or information. As for the source of their manifesting properties, when you think about it crystals are creative energy in physical form. The minerals that created these crystals came from ancient Stars and Planets as they were still forming. Many crystals are thousands if not millions of years old. Some grew billions of years ago and are older than all life on Earth.

Crystals contain elements that are a fundamental part of all life on Earth, such as Iron and Silica. Crystals are crystallised seeds of creative energy. The alchemical process that created these crystals deep within Earth's fiery furnace, can be tapped into for manifestation work.

From the spiritual point of view, crystals also act as catalysts. They alter the vibration of energies around you or within you, to create change in your life. They can be programmed for specific needs and desires. The crystals that are used in a Crystal Grid are selected to carry the types of energies needed for a situation. They can be seen as the power source or batteries of a Crystal Grid. Some crystals are used to amplify or broadcast these energies out into the Universe or towards a person or place.

Even the forms of crystals used such as Crystal Points, Double Terminated Crystals or Crystal Pyramids all have their own purpose and way of directing energies. We will be looking at this in more detail later on.

The physical structure of the crystal also acts as an anchor point for energies. The Crystal Grid becomes a physical yet symbolic representation of the intention behind it. This structure also acts as a visual reminder of the purpose behind the grid. It speaks to us both consciously and at a subconscious level.

## Sacred Geometry

Sacred Geometry is the belief in the spiritual or divine significance and power of geometry. These geometric shapes, which exist everywhere from our cells to the Galaxies, are seen to represent the fingerprint of the divine. They are like the framework for creation and all life. Without geometry there would be no manifested world or life forms.

In recent years Sacred Geometry has become more and more explored outside of esoteric groups. This subject is vast and encompasses ancient cultures, traditions, religions, architecture, genetics, biology, physics, astrophysics, spirituality, cosmology, numerology and philosophy. Hundreds of books have been written about it and whole volumes could be written about just one of the key geometric shapes. If you look, Sacred Geometry is the basis of nearly all Crystal Grid designs. They are not just to look symmetrical or appear mystical.

As already explained the crystalline structure of most minerals is geometric. The formations of certain crystals such as Quartz crystals show clear geometric shapes. These geometries form part of the synergistic power of Crystal Grids. The shapes and microscopic geometric patterns of crystals help form the energetic blueprint behind Crystal Grids.

Sacred Geometry is used to align with greater energies such as those of the Earth and the Universe. Crystals are arranged into these shapes to plug into these geometric energy fields and focus the energies of the crystals towards a desired result. Tapping into the Earth's energy field and Ley Lines helps manifest things in the Physical World, where they are needed.

By using Sacred Geometry you are also making sure that your desire or goal is in alignment with that of the Universe and the greater plan or purpose for your life.

## Numerology

Numerology is the metaphysical science of numbers and their meaning. The belief in the spiritual significance of numbers is also ancient and can be found in many cultures, religions and traditions all around the world.

Although most people are more familiar with numerology being applied to names and birth dates for personality and destiny analysis, it has lots of other applications. The symbolic meaning of numbers has been used in Temples, religious, magical or shamanic ceremonies, dream interpretation and art.

Numerology is closely related and some would say the very root of Sacred Geometry. A single point in space becomes two, forming a line. Add another point to make three and we get the first geometric shape, the triangle. The symbolic meaning of numbers is very similar to that of their related geometric shapes. In a Crystal Grid we would use three crystals to form a triangle, so naturally the number three and the triangle both hold a very similar significance and power that you may want to tap into.

## Manifesting

Manifesting is a metaphysical term used to describe the process of creating something in your life or the world. This could be drawing a situation, opportunity, new job or significant person into your life.

This is based on the belief that all humans have a spiritual creative power. That we can attract things into our life, if we focus on them. Everything around us is made of energy, including ourselves. So it makes sense that employing the right use and amount of energy could attract something or change things in our life. These energetic changes are believed to influence the Physical World around us, which is made of energy too.

There is now a lot of information, techniques and methods to manifest things out there. Crystal Grids are just one way. You will be programming or infusing your crystals and the grid with your desired intention. These energies are meant to alter the energy of a situation, open new doors to change or attract your wishes. Crystal Grids do go beyond the world of just manifesting our goals like creating better finances for example. They can be used to create a peaceful environment, bring healing or receive divine guidance for example. The possibilities are endless.

## Your Intention

As with all aspects of Crystal Healing, I believe that your intention is what is going to really matter the most. Having a clear intention as to what it is you want to manifest or happen is essential. Really think about what it is that you want and why you want it. Be sure this is something that you would like to happen in your life and that you are prepared to really act on this, should it happen.

The Crystal Grids in this book are designed for different purposes, but see them as guides. They can always be personalised for your unique situation. Being clear about exactly what it is you wish to happen is going to really help you a lot.

Although it is also worth remembering not to be too specific that we limit ourselves. This can happen if we state exactly how we think the outcome will manifest. Watch that you are not too rigid or controlling that you actually block opportunities or something that is even better than you dreamed. You should try to avoid things like "I will get x amount of money by this time next month through the sale of my House". It would be better to say, "My Home will sell with ease".

I will give you a suggestion for the wording of your statement of intention for each of the grids, which you can use to base yourself on. You can use these as they are or adapt them for your specific needs. Always remember these are your words of power so keep them positive, clear and empowering.

I believe we are more like co-creators with the divine, manifesting is not as simple as some have made out. There are lots of factors involved and timing is not something that can be easily controlled by anyone. The important thing is to be clear about what you want but not too specific about 'how' exactly it will happen. Your crystal clear intention will program the Crystal Grid and make sure that it is in alignment with your goal.

The other thing that can take all your manifestation work to the next level is using visualisation. While you are programming your crystals with your intention, you want to really see it and feel it as if it were manifested already. Visualise your desired result and all the blessings that it brings to you and to others involved.

Charge this vision by feeling all the positive emotions like joy, satisfaction and peace you would feel if it were happening now. For something like healing, see the person in perfect health. For an end to arguments in the Home, see everyone getting along again and feel the good energy filling your House.

Your vision and emotions add power to your Crystal Grids. They imprint the energy with more clarity on how this could look and how you or others want to feel. This is not always conveyed in words. If you struggle with this part you may need to consider why you are creating the Crystal Grid. Make sure you are not manifesting something that you think you should have.

As with anything like this it is worth also remembering to make sure that your use of Crystal Grids is ethical. If you alter the purpose of a grid here or create your own, make sure that it is not in any way trying to control another person or cause harm. It is always best to ask someone for permission if you want to use a Crystal Grid to help them with things like protection or healing.

Although you may mean well, you need to get permission. There may be valid exceptions, such as when a person is unable to communicate after an accident or illness for example.

This is a very personal thing that will vary from person to person. Only you can decide what is right for you. It's a good idea to add to your intention that the healing or protection be sent to someone only if it is for their highest good. This makes sure that you are not doing anything that you should not be doing or violating anyone's free will. I have inbuilt this into the intention statements for the Crystal Grids in this book for you.

## A Complete & Balanced Approach

It's important to remember that no matter what you do on an energetic or spiritual level, you must also take physical action where possible. Crystal Grids can help you manifest your goals and make changes but should not be used as a substitute for the time and work needed to get to where you want to be. Crystal Grids are not a magic bullet for all your problems.

The Universe does not work like a microwave meal. Things may take time to manifest. Although we have all heard stories of people that asked for something to come into their lives and then it happened the next day, this is not normal. If you created a Crystal Grid for a better paid job but do not actually apply for any jobs, there is very little chance you will be offered one. This is because your actions do not align with your intentions.

When you take the armchair approach to manifestation, you are sending very mixed signals to the Universe. If you're not prepared to put any effort or energy into getting that job, then why should the Universe help you? How much do you really want it? If you want something to happen you need to do as much as you possibly can to make it happen. You want to take spiritual action through the Crystal Grid. Take mental and emotional action by staying focused and positive about your goal. Take physical action by doing what needs to be done to get to where you want to be.

## The Crystal Grid Diamond

To summarise how Crystal Grids work take a look at the following diagram. This diamond shows the different facets of energy that are used to crystallise your intentions into reality. Crystal Healing, Sacred Geometry, Numerology, Intention and Action in the centre.

All these forces need to be working together. Without a clear intention or purposeful action, the diamond is broken and incomplete.

# Chapter 13 Care of Crystals

When a crystal is obtained, the first important thing to do is to cleanse the crystal. Crystals are natural energy absorbers, and to cleanse them means to remove previous energy from them. The process of cleansing is important not only in the beginning but after every time the holder uses the crystals. Stones need to be revitalized and recharged in order to work.

There are many different ways to recognize when a crystal needs to be cleansed. Some stones such as quartz tend to become cloudy. Some crystals lose their brightness and clairvoyance, while others manifest other physical changes, for example, they become heavier. The crystals that are placed in the house or used as accessories have to be cleaned often, and that also depends on how much are they used. This kind of stone, when charged, doesn't emit any special energy, it just provides the feeling of willpower and the decisiveness to succeed. When this happens, cleanse the crystal, and the crystal will feel just as brand new as before.

There are a few methods for cleansing crystals, here are some of the most common ones:

The first one is to cleanse the crystal using the energy of the holder. This kind of cleansing is achieved through clear intention and a focused mind. The holder needs to visualize that the crystal is immersed in the white light while holding the crystal, and keep visualizing the purification of bad energy as well as its recharge. This process should last for a few minutes, and when completed, the energy inside the crystal will have transformed into a positive and pure one and that the crystal now has its full potential.

Another way is to cleanse the crystal is with water. The crystal should be put under a tap, and it should be washed with cold water. For the process to work, the holder must visualize that the negative energy is dissolved in the water and that it is washed away from the crystal. The visualization should continue by imagining the transformation of dissolved negative energy into the positive, healing one. When the water has washed away this visualized energy and transformed it into the positive one, the impurities of the crystal should have disappeared and the crystal is once again, ready to use. If the crystals, however, are washed in the rain or somewhere else in nature, it is important to keep in mind that the stone must be dried naturally - the best way would be to put them in a sunny spot.

There is a third way to cleanse the crystals, and it is mostly used by dedicated practitioners who enjoy exotic scents and understand the importance of crystal care. The crystal is cleansed by using the smoke of herbs that are considered to be sacred. In this case, those herbs can be lavender, sage, cedar, and so forth, and their smoke is used to smudge the energetic matrix of crystals and consequently, cleanse them. Smudging the crystals using white sage removes negativity away from the crystals. In essence, smudging is a process of lighting these sacred herbs and burning them. When the flame of these plants dies, the embers stay, burn, and they create smoke. The crystal is put through this smoke with the intent to be purified.

Crystals can be put on a rock salt bed for 48 hours and cleansed by the purifying rock salt. They can also be cleansed slowly by being buried into the soil. This process lasts two to seven days.

Crystals should never be washed with hot water. Water should always be from a tap and washing under water is not recommended for crystals such as opals, pearls, or turquoise since they can be damaged in the water due to their structure. It is also recommended not to use chlorinated water since it can also damage the crystals.

As previously explained, there are many ways to cleanse the crystals. However, after they are cleaned, they need to be recharged. Here are a few ways to recharge the crystals:

The first way is to place the crystal in sunlight for a few hours. This technique is used to recharge most stones. After leaving it for some time under the sun, the crystal will have a brighter color. For a full and complete recharge, the crystal should be placed on the earth so it can connect with the sun, the moon, and the stars.

The second way to recharge a crystal is to leave the stone under the moon, ideally a full moon. The moon has a great influence on the stones and gives them an even greater charge.

Crystals can be charged if they are put out in some dynamic weather conditions. If the crystal is charged during a thunderstorm, for example, it would give the stone a strong electromagnetic charge.

Crystals are fragile so it is important to treat them with care. They can chip and get damaged so it is recommended to have a separate bag for them if you are traveling. If the holder wants to unlock their full potential by using the crystals outside, stones should be handled with care and put on some silk or satin material. The location must also be carefully selected. Use the crystals in a dry area; there should not be moisture or you should not be in conditions that could damage or break the stones.

If the holder has crystals that are really expensive and hard to obtain, they should use boxes built from materials that are acid-free, otherwise, there is risk of a chemical reaction. Small fragments that are fragile should be kept in separate containers - an economical way would be to use egg cartons for storage. It is important to keep the harder and softer stones separate as the harder stones could damage the soft ones.

All crystals are unique. They should be handled with care because they represent one point in time and one stage of earth's geological development. Some gemstones are more expensive than others, but that doesn't mean that their spiritual worth is lesser. They are all a part of the process and should be treated as such.

## Different Colored Crystals And Their Significance

It might all be quite fascinating if you're using crystals for the first time. They not only offer spiritual healing powers, but are also a great way to build a connection with the energy given off by the crystals. There are several types of crystals, and each of these crystals means a different thing. Each crystal is unique, and their powers are unique too. The color of the crystal is one of the factors that must be taken into consideration while selecting a crystal. The power of the crystal, when combined with the frequency of the color, tends to create a certain effect. It is quintessential that you understand this before you start selecting crystals.

Since you're just getting started with learning about crystals, understanding the colors and the significance is a great way to start. Also, don't forget that when it comes to crystals, trusting your intuition matters more than the color, shape, or even the type of the crystal. If you know what you are seeking, you will find that you are not drawn to the crystal. So, a little awareness will certainly come in handy. The colors of different chakras tend to resonate with one of the colors of the seven chakras or the energy centers in your body. Each of these energy centers is responsible for your physical, or will, and emotional well-being. In this section, you will learn about the significance of different colored crystals.

White-colored crystals

White crystals are said to signify purity and peace. White or clear crystals tend to emit energy, which is believed to be cleansing and purifying. For instance, clear quartz can be used for amplifying the energy of other crystals, whereas selenite can be used for cleansing any space. Likewise, moonstone can be used for removing any tensions or negative emotions from an individual. Apart from this, white crystals or clear crystals are quite easy to work with and connect with. They promote an overall sense of peace and serenity. They are also a great tool to be used while meditating or doing any sort of energy-cleansing work.

The different examples of white or clear crystals include moonstone, selenite, clear quartz, white chalcedony, and apophyllite.

Black-colored crystals

Black crystals are considered to be extremely powerful when it comes to offering protection. If you want to banish negativity from your life and your surroundings, then using black crystals is a great idea. Whenever you need to protect yourself and safeguard your mental health, then these crystals are helpful. Safety and security are the two things provided by black stones or crystals. They can quickly dispel your fears and start creating a sense of security and safety. Security and safety are not just related to your physical health, but your mental and spiritual health too. Since they shield you from so much negativity, they are referred to as barrier crystals. Not only do they offer these protective abilities, but barrier crystals also help improve the wearer's focus while amplifying their efforts to keep away any negativity.

White stones tend to help reflect purifying light, whereas black-colored stones can absorb light. It can also be used for unlocking any hidden talent or potential within an individual. Black is said to be a solidifying color. It is believed that black crystals have tremendous power stored within them, and you need a little patience to unlock it. The different examples of black crystals include obsidian, shungite, black tourmaline, and black kyanite.

Red-colored crystals

If you're looking for a crystal that will make you feel energized and pumped up, then these crystals will do the trick. Do you every use the clever drink red bull or any other energy drink? Don't you feel revitalized or unauthorized? Likewise, red crystals perform the same function. Red is a color that is associated with our life force, the planet Mars, and the root chakra. Our life force, or blood, and the planet Mars are associated with war, passion, and sex. The root chakra guides our basic animalistic instincts. So, it is no wonder that the energy given out by red-colored crystals is raw and intense. It is believed that red crystals will give you the determination and the motivation that's necessary to keep going. So, if you need to boost your energy or get actively involved in something, then opt for red stones.

The different examples of red-colored crystals include garnet, ruby, red jasper, rubellite, and vanadinite.

Orange-colored crystals

Orange crystals help to combine energy with focus. Therefore, these crystals are believed to promote creativity as well as artistic skills in an individual. This color is also associated with the sacral chakra. So, orange is believed to be associated with creativity as well as sexuality. These crystals can provide a source of energy and inspire creativity. If you feel like you need to make things a little more interesting for yourself, then these crystals will certainly come in handy. Also, these crystals are believed to be quite helpful in general as they act as catalysts or supporters of any major life changes. So, if you're looking for swift decision-making, then you can start working with these crystals.

One of the most popular orange-colored stones is carnelian. Carnelian is believed to project warmth and there are various instances throughout history about how carnelian was favored by the pharaohs of ancient Egypt. Different examples of orange-colored crystals include amber, sunstone, carnelian, orange calcite, and sunset aura quartz.

Pink-colored crystals

The energy radiated by pink crystals tends to feel like a warm hug for your heart. Its gentle, soothing, warm, and loving energy can make anyone feel good. Pink crystals tend to promote feelings of calmness and compassion. It is believed that these crystals bring love and kindness into the life of its wearer. These crystals can be used for matters related to love, forgiveness, kindness, self-love, emotional healing, or anything else along these lines. If you want to open up your heart and let others in or connect with others, then start using pink-colored crystals.

Emotions and sensitivity, along with subtle and gentle energies, can be incorporated into your life by using crystals of this color. One of the most popular pink-colored stones is the rose quartz. Any suppressed or unexpressed emotions can be quite a hindrance to your personal growth and you can use rose quartz to prevent this from happening. By using pink crystals, you can unleash or let go of such suppressed energies. These stones are also associated with unconditional love and self-love.

Pink tourmaline, rose quartz, pink opal, rhodonite, and rhodochrosite are all examples of pink crystals.

Yellow-colored crystals

The color associated with the solar plexus chakra is yellow. The energy given out by yellow-colored crystals is quite similar to the energy of the solar plexus chakra. Yellow is also associated with the color of the sun. Just the way a sun shines brightly and gives off energy that can fill anyone with warmth, yellow-colored crystals tend to do the same. It is also believed that these crystals are associated with your digestive system, nervous system, and the immune system.

The energy of these crystals is bright and optimistic. Apart from this, it will also help you find your true self. The solar plexus chakra is related to your sense of self, so yellow crystals can inspire self-confidence. If you want to feel good and experience a boost in confidence, then yellow crystals can help.

Sulfur quartz, citrine, golden onyx, yellow jasper, and honey calcite are all examples of yellow-colored crystals.

Blue-colored crystals

The color blue is associated with two chakras in your body. Light blue is associated with the throat chakra, whereas indigo is associated with the third eye chakra. The throat chakra is representative of all forms of communication, and therefore, light blue is representative of the same. Your senses of touch, taste, smell, sight, and the ability to feel are all related to the color blue.

Apart from this, all of your internal communication processes, such as the way you talk to yourself and express your thoughts, are influenced by the energy of these stones. Peace of mind, intuition, perception, and the ability to understand are associated with indigo. The way the ocean or the sky tends to have a soothing and calming effect, blue-colored crystals also have that same effect on your body. Blue crystals can bring about clarity and enable you to be your most authentic self. You can do all this while staying calm, composed, and collected.

Lapis lazuli, aquamarine, azurite, blue lace agate, and larimar are examples of blue-colored crystals.

Green-colored crystals

Green is the color of nature as well as money. If you're looking at making a fresh beginning and want to enable the growth of your spirit, then connecting to a green crystal is a good idea. Green crystals like jade are often used for attracting prosperity, wealth, and money. They are considered to be sacred stones in Asia.

Green is also associated with the heart chakra. Green colored crystals can be used to establish balance as well as stability in all relationships and an individual's emotions. It is representative of your personal growth and serendipity. Apart from this, green crystals can also help in getting rid of any feelings of anxiety or stress while inciting happiness and joyful attitude towards life. If you want to break free of any toxic relationships or harmful behavior patterns, green crystals can help. By bringing about stability to matters of heart, it will certainly improve your overall sense of well-being.

Moss agate, green aventurine, jade, and malachite are examples of green-colored crystals.

Purple or violet-colored crystals

Violet is the color associated with the crown chakra or the seventh chakra. Violet crystals can help you tap into feelings of inspiration, empathy, and also give you a sense of service to those around you. These stones can help bring balance in extreme situations. Also, you can use them whenever you are unsure of the nature of the problem that you are facing in life. Purple crystals are believed to be quite spiritual and can help in bringing about balance to your spiritual side. They can not only help you find inspiration, but also enable you to tap into the divine forces of the cosmos. If you want to find your true purpose in life, then these crystals are the ones to use. Purple or violet colored crystals and stones are often used for practicing meditation.

Amethyst, sugilite, lepidolite, charoite, and spirit quartz are all examples of purple crystals.

# Conclusion

Congratulations on your journey through the chakras and learning all you need to know about how to begin healing your own energy! This book is a welcoming resource for you to start practicing the healing process and with all of your new knowledge about chakras, you can begin to explore in a more in-depth way on your own. Your intuition is all you need now, to help you achieve the level of balance and vibrational flow required to feel that wholeness and enlightenment that comes from an unblocked and healthy chakra system.

This book has shown you the beautiful history and discovery of the chakras as well as an understanding of how we can use modern science to explore and explain what is really happening on the energetic level with our bodies. The connection between the chakras and the physical/emotional self is strong and I hope that you can now see how dynamic our total being truly is within that mind-body-spirit balance.

You have taken a unique road trip through the chakra system and learned about how each of them has distinct qualities and characteristics that set them apart from each other, and how all together, they create a uniform wholeness that leads to the transcendent self and connection to the truth and purpose of your life.

All of the information in this book is here to show you what kinds of ailments, issues and challenges can present themselves when your chakras are unhealthy, blocked and imbalanced. As you move forward, you can begin to identify these causes and side-effects in your own life and begin to energetically treat yourself through the healing process.

You have all of the techniques outlined for you to get started and any number of them will shift and transform your energy the more you practice them. Remember that daily or weekly energy clearing, using any of these methods, will keep you in a better balance overall.

The goal of this book is to show you how to work with your chakra energy for a fuller, happier, healthier life and how-to bring positivity into your vibration and frequency more regularly. The power of living in balance will bring into you harmony with the life you have always wanted to live. Moving forward, keep your energy open and flowing using these chakra healing techniques and the knowledge you have gained about your own, unique energy system.

Everything that you do in your life, and every person you encounter, will influence your energy and your chakras. We carry this energy around with us, sometimes for our whole lives and if you are wanting to heal the wounds of the past, traumatic circumstances, chronic health problems, emotional challenges and upheaval, to create a more balanced and energetically vibrant life, then all you have to do is listen to your energy and "read" your chakras.

Refer to this book as often as you need to in order to stay focused on your healing path. You can use it as a platform to get you started and to lead you into even deeper knowledge about how all of your chakras work to balance each other out. Bring this knowledge into your every day self-care routines and practices and watch your life transform.

CPSIA information can be obtained
at www.ICGtesting.com
Printed in the USA
BVHW090923170321
602755BV00009B/507

9 781838 317805